THE SCARLET LETTER

Nathaniel Hawthorne

SPARK PUBLISHING

SPARKNOTES is a registered trademark of SparkNotes LLC

Spark Publishing
A Division of Barnes & Noble
120 Fifth Avenue
New York, NY 10011
www.sparknotes.com

ISBN-13: 978-1-4114-0322-2
ISBN-10: 1-4114-0322-3

Please submit changes or report errors to www.sparknotes.com/errors.

Printed in the United States.

10 9 8 7 6 5 4 3 2 1

Contents

NOTE: This study guide was prepared using the Bantam Classic edition of *The Scarlet Letter*. Hawthorne apparently burned the novel's manuscript; thus, his original intentions have been difficult to reconstuct. Most available editions of the novel have been prepared from its first American edition and are quite similar to one another. Any differences among other American-edition-based printings will likely have to do with spelling and punctuation changes, and with substitutions for a few words missing from the first American edition. Plot details and chapter organization should be the same.

CONTEXT

NATHANIEL HAWTHORNE WAS BORN in Salem, Massachusetts, in 1804. His family descended from the earliest settlers of the Massachusetts Bay Colony; among his forebearers was John Hathorne (Hawthorne added the "w" to his name when he began to write), one of the judges at the 1692 Salem witch trials. Throughout his life, Hawthorne was both fascinated and disturbed by his kinship with John Hathorne. Raised by a widowed mother, Hawthorne attended Bowdoin College in Maine, where he met two people who were to have great impact upon his life: Henry Wadsworth Longfellow, who would later become a famous poet, and Franklin Pierce, who would later become president of the United States.

After college Hawthorne tried his hand at writing, producing historical sketches and an anonymous novel, *Fanshawe,* that detailed his college days rather embarrassingly. Hawthorne also held positions as an editor and as a customs surveyor during this period. His growing relationship with the intellectual circle that included Ralph Waldo Emerson and Margaret Fuller led him to abandon his customs post for the utopian experiment at Brook Farm, a commune designed to promote economic self-sufficiency and transcendentalist principles. Transcendentalism was a religious and philosophical movement of the early nineteenth century that was dedicated to the belief that divinity manifests itself everywhere, particularly in the natural world. It also advocated a personalized, direct relationship with the divine in place of formalized, structured religion. This second transcendental idea is privileged in *The Scarlet Letter.*

After marrying fellow transcendentalist Sophia Peabody in 1842, Hawthorne left Brook Farm and moved into the Old Manse, a home in Concord where Emerson had once lived. In 1846 he published *Mosses from an Old Manse,* a collection of essays and stories, many of which are about early America. *Mosses from an Old Manse* earned Hawthorne the attention of the literary establishment because America was trying to establish a cultural independence to complement its political independence, and Hawthorne's collection of stories displayed both a stylistic freshness and an interest in American subject matter. Herman Melville, among others, hailed Hawthorne as the "American Shakespeare."

In 1845 Hawthorne again went to work as a customs surveyor, this time, like the narrator of *The Scarlet Letter*, at a post in Salem. In 1850, after having lost the job, he published *The Scarlet Letter* to enthusiastic, if not widespread, acclaim. His other major novels include *The House of the Seven Gables* (1851), *The Blithedale Romance* (1852), and *The Marble Faun* (1860). In 1853 Hawthorne's college friend Franklin Pierce, for whom he had written a campaign biography and who had since become president, appointed Hawthorne a United States consul. The writer spent the next six years in Europe. He died in 1864, a few years after returning to America.

The majority of Hawthorne's work takes America's Puritan past as its subject, but *The Scarlet Letter* uses the material to greatest effect. The Puritans were a group of religious reformers who arrived in Massachusetts in the 1630s under the leadership of John Winthrop (whose death is recounted in the novel). The religious sect was known for its intolerance of dissenting ideas and lifestyles. In *The Scarlet Letter,* Hawthorne uses the repressive, authoritarian Puritan society as an analogue for humankind in general. The Puritan setting also enables him to portray the human soul under extreme pressures. Hester, Dimmesdale, and Chillingworth, while unquestionably part of the Puritan society in which they live, also reflect universal experiences. Hawthorne speaks specifically to American issues, but he circumvents the aesthetic and thematic limitations that might accompany such a focus. His universality and his dramatic flair have ensured his place in the literary canon.

PLOT OVERVIEW

THE SCARLET LETTER OPENS with a long preamble about how the book came to be written. The nameless narrator was the surveyor of the customhouse in Salem, Massachusetts. In the customhouse's attic, he discovered a number of documents, among them a manuscript that was bundled with a scarlet, gold-embroidered patch of cloth in the shape of an "A." The manuscript, the work of a past surveyor, detailed events that occurred some two hundred years before the narrator's time. When the narrator lost his customs post, he decided to write a fictional account of the events recorded in the manuscript. *The Scarlet Letter* is the final product.

The story begins in seventeenth-century Boston, then a Puritan settlement. A young woman, Hester Prynne, is led from the town prison with her infant daughter, Pearl, in her arms and the scarlet letter "A" on her breast. A man in the crowd tells an elderly onlooker that Hester is being punished for adultery. Hester's husband, a scholar much older than she is, sent her ahead to America, but he never arrived in Boston. The consensus is that he has been lost at sea. While waiting for her husband, Hester has apparently had an affair, as she has given birth to a child. She will not reveal her lover's identity, however, and the scarlet letter, along with her public shaming, is her punishment for her sin and her secrecy. On this day Hester is led to the town scaffold and harangued by the town fathers, but she again refuses to identify her child's father.

The elderly onlooker is Hester's missing husband, who is now practicing medicine and calling himself Roger Chillingworth. He settles in Boston, intent on revenge. He reveals his true identity to no one but Hester, whom he has sworn to secrecy. Several years pass. Hester supports herself by working as a seamstress, and Pearl grows into a willful, impish child. Shunned by the community, they live in a small cottage on the outskirts of Boston. Community officials attempt to take Pearl away from Hester, but, with the help of Arthur Dimmesdale, a young and eloquent minister, the mother and daughter manage to stay together. Dimmesdale, however, appears to be wasting away and suffers from mysterious heart trouble, seemingly caused by psychological distress. Chillingworth attaches himself to the ailing minister and eventually moves in with him so that he can provide

3

his patient with round-the-clock care. Chillingworth also suspects that there may be a connection between the minister's torments and Hester's secret, and he begins to test Dimmesdale to see what he can learn. One afternoon, while the minister sleeps, Chillingworth discovers a mark on the man's breast (the details of which are kept from the reader), which convinces him that his suspicions are correct.

Dimmesdale's psychological anguish deepens, and he invents new tortures for himself. In the meantime, Hester's charitable deeds and quiet humility have earned her a reprieve from the scorn of the community. One night, when Pearl is about seven years old, she and her mother are returning home from a visit to a deathbed when they encounter Dimmesdale atop the town scaffold, trying to punish himself for his sins. Hester and Pearl join him, and the three link hands. Dimmesdale refuses Pearl's request that he acknowledge her publicly the next day, and a meteor marks a dull red "A" in the night sky. Hester can see that the minister's condition is worsening, and she resolves to intervene. She goes to Chillingworth and asks him to stop adding to Dimmesdale's self-torment. Chillingworth refuses.

Hester arranges an encounter with Dimmesdale in the forest because she is aware that Chillingworth has probably guessed that she plans to reveal his identity to Dimmesdale. The former lovers decide to flee to Europe, where they can live with Pearl as a family. They will take a ship sailing from Boston in four days. Both feel a sense of release, and Hester removes her scarlet letter and lets down her hair. Pearl, playing nearby, does not recognize her mother without the letter. The day before the ship is to sail, the townspeople gather for a holiday and Dimmesdale preaches his most eloquent sermon ever. Meanwhile, Hester has learned that Chillingworth knows of their plan and has booked passage on the same ship. Dimmesdale, leaving the church after his sermon, sees Hester and Pearl standing before the town scaffold. He impulsively mounts the scaffold with his lover and his daughter, and confesses publicly, exposing a scarlet letter seared into the flesh of his chest. He falls dead, as Pearl kisses him.

Frustrated in his revenge, Chillingworth dies a year later. Hester and Pearl leave Boston, and no one knows what has happened to them. Many years later, Hester returns alone, still wearing the scarlet letter, to live in her old cottage and resume her charitable work. She receives occasional letters from Pearl, who has married a European aristocrat and established a family of her own. When Hester dies, she is buried next to Dimmesdale. The two share a single tombstone, which bears a scarlet "A."

CHARACTER LIST

Hester Prynne Hester is the book's protagonist and the wearer of the scarlet letter that gives the book its title. The letter, a patch of fabric in the shape of an "A," signifies that Hester is an "adulterer." As a young woman, Hester married an elderly scholar, Chillingworth, who sent her ahead to America to live but never followed her. While waiting for him, she had an affair with a Puritan minister named Dimmesdale, after which she gave birth to Pearl. Hester is passionate but also strong—she endures years of shame and scorn. She equals both her husband and her lover in her intelligence and thoughtfulness. Her alienation puts her in the position to make acute observations about her community, particularly about its treatment of women.

Pearl Hester's illegitimate daughter Pearl is a young girl with a moody, mischievous spirit and an ability to perceive things that others do not. For example, she quickly discerns the truth about her mother and Dimmesdale. The townspeople say that she barely seems human and spread rumors that her unknown father is actually the Devil. She is wise far beyond her years, frequently engaging in ironic play having to do with her mother's scarlet letter.

Roger Chillingworth "Roger Chillingworth" is actually Hester's husband in disguise. He is much older than she is and had sent her to America while he settled his affairs in Europe. Because he is captured by Native Americans, he arrives in Boston belatedly and finds Hester and her illegitimate child being displayed on the scaffold. He lusts for revenge, and thus decides to stay in Boston despite his wife's betrayal and disgrace. He is a scholar and uses his knowledge to disguise himself as a doctor, intent on discovering and tormenting Hester's anonymous lover. Chillingworth is self-absorbed and both physically and psychologically monstrous. His single-minded pursuit of retribution reveals him to be the most malevolent character in the novel.

Reverend Arthur Dimmesdale Dimmesdale is a young man who achieved fame in England as a theologian and then emigrated to America. In a moment of weakness, he and Hester became lovers. Although he will not confess it publicly, he is the father of her child. He deals with his guilt by tormenting himself physically and psychologically, developing a heart condition as a result. Dimmesdale is an intelligent and emotional man, and his sermons are thus masterpieces of eloquence and persuasiveness. His commitments to his congregation are in constant conflict with his feelings of sinfulness and need to confess.

Governor Bellingham Governor Bellingham is a wealthy, elderly gentleman who spends much of his time consulting with the other town fathers. Despite his role as governor of a fledgling American society, he very much resembles a traditional English aristocrat. Bellingham tends to strictly adhere to the rules, but he is easily swayed by Dimmesdale's eloquence. He remains blind to the misbehaviors taking place in his own house: his sister, Mistress Hibbins, is a witch.

Mistress Hibbins Mistress Hibbins is a widow who lives with her brother, Governor Bellingham, in a luxurious mansion. She is commonly known to be a witch who ventures into the forest at night to ride with the "Black Man." Her appearances at public occasions remind the reader of the hypocrisy and hidden evil in Puritan society.

Reverend Mr. John Wilson Boston's elder clergyman, Reverend Wilson is scholarly yet grandfatherly. He is a stereotypical Puritan father, a literary version of the stiff, starkly painted portraits of American patriarchs. Like Governor Bellingham, Wilson follows the community's rules strictly but can be swayed by Dimmesdale's eloquence. Unlike Dimmesdale, his junior colleague, Wilson preaches hellfire and damnation and advocates harsh punishment of sinners.

Narrator   The unnamed narrator works as the surveyor of the Salem Custom House some two hundred years after the novel's events take place. He discovers an old manuscript in the building's attic that tells the story of Hester Prynne; when he loses his job, he decides to write a fictional treatment of the narrative. The narrator is a rather high-strung man, whose Puritan ancestry makes him feel guilty about his writing career. He writes because he is interested in American history and because he believes that America needs to better understand its religious and moral heritage.

ANALYSIS OF MAJOR CHARACTERS

HESTER PRYNNE

Although *The Scarlet Letter* is about Hester Prynne, the book is not so much a consideration of her innate character as it is an examination of the forces that shape her and the transformations those forces effect. We know very little about Hester prior to her affair with Dimmesdale and her resultant public shaming. We read that she married Chillingworth although she did not love him, but we never fully understand why. The early chapters of the book suggest that, prior to her marriage, Hester was a strong-willed and impetuous young woman—she remembers her parents as loving guides who frequently had to restrain her incautious behavior. The fact that she has an affair also suggests that she once had a passionate nature.

But it is what happens after Hester's affair that makes her into the woman with whom the reader is familiar. Shamed and alienated from the rest of the community, Hester becomes contemplative. She speculates on human nature, social organization, and larger moral questions. Hester's tribulations also lead her to be stoic and a free-thinker. Although the narrator pretends to disapprove of Hester's independent philosophizing, his tone indicates that he secretly admires her independence and her ideas.

Hester also becomes a kind of compassionate maternal figure as a result of her experiences. Hester moderates her tendency to be rash, for she knows that such behavior could cause her to lose her daughter, Pearl. Hester is also maternal with respect to society: she cares for the poor and brings them food and clothing. By the novel's end, Hester has become a protofeminist mother figure to the women of the community. The shame attached to her scarlet letter is long gone. Women recognize that her punishment stemmed in part from the town fathers' sexism, and they come to Hester seeking shelter from the sexist forces under which they themselves suffer. Throughout *The Scarlet Letter* Hester is portrayed as an intelligent, capable, but not necessarily extraordinary woman. It is the extraordinary circumstances shaping her that make her such an important figure.

Roger Chillingworth

As his name suggests, Roger Chillingworth is a man deficient in human warmth. His twisted, stooped, deformed shoulders mirror his distorted soul. From what the reader is told of his early years with Hester, he was a difficult husband. He ignored his wife for much of the time, yet expected her to nourish his soul with affection when he did condescend to spend time with her. Chillingworth's decision to assume the identity of a "leech," or doctor, is fitting. Unable to engage in equitable relationships with those around him, he feeds on the vitality of others as a way of energizing his own projects. Chillingworth's death is a result of the nature of his character. After Dimmesdale dies, Chillingworth no longer has a victim. Similarly, Dimmesdale's revelation that he is Pearl's father removes Hester from the old man's clutches. Having lost the objects of his revenge, the leech has no choice but to die.

Ultimately, Chillingworth represents true evil. He is associated with secular and sometimes illicit forms of knowledge, as his chemical experiments and medical practices occasionally verge on witchcraft and murder. He is interested in revenge, not justice, and he seeks the deliberate destruction of others rather than a redress of wrongs. His desire to hurt others stands in contrast to Hester and Dimmesdale's sin, which had love, not hate, as its intent. Any harm that may have come from the young lovers' deed was unanticipated and inadvertent, whereas Chillingworth reaps deliberate harm.

Arthur Dimmesdale

Arthur Dimmesdale, like Hester Prynne, is an individual whose identity owes more to external circumstances than to his innate nature. The reader is told that Dimmesdale was a scholar of some renown at Oxford University. His past suggests that he is probably somewhat aloof, the kind of man who would not have much natural sympathy for ordinary men and women. However, Dimmesdale has an unusually active conscience. The fact that Hester takes all of the blame for their shared sin goads his conscience, and his resultant mental anguish and physical weakness open up his mind and allow him to empathize with others. Consequently, he becomes an eloquent and emotionally powerful speaker and a compassionate leader, and his congregation is able to receive meaningful spiritual guidance from him.

Ironically, the townspeople do not believe Dimmesdale's protestations of sinfulness. Given his background and his penchant for rhetorical speech, Dimmesdale's congregation generally interprets his sermons allegorically rather than as expressions of any personal guilt. This drives Dimmesdale to further internalize his guilt and self-punishment and leads to still more deterioration in his physical and spiritual condition. The town's idolization of him reaches new heights after his Election Day sermon, which is his last. In his death, Dimmesdale becomes even more of an icon than he was in life. Many believe his confession was a symbolic act, while others believe Dimmesdale's fate was an example of divine judgment.

PEARL

Hester's daughter, Pearl, functions primarily as a symbol. She is quite young during most of the events of this novel—when Dimmesdale dies she is only seven years old—and her real importance lies in her ability to provoke the adult characters in the book. She asks them pointed questions and draws their attention, and the reader's, to the denied or overlooked truths of the adult world. In general, children in *The Scarlet Letter* are portrayed as more perceptive and more honest than adults, and Pearl is the most perceptive of them all.

Pearl makes us constantly aware of her mother's scarlet letter and of the society that produced it. From an early age, she fixates on the emblem. Pearl's innocent, or perhaps intuitive, comments about the letter raise crucial questions about its meaning. Similarly, she inquires about the relationships between those around her—most important, the relationship between Hester and Dimmesdale—and offers perceptive critiques of them. Pearl provides the text's harshest, and most penetrating, judgment of Dimmesdale's failure to admit to his adultery. Once her father's identity is revealed, Pearl is no longer needed in this symbolic capacity; at Dimmesdale's death she becomes fully "human," leaving behind her otherworldliness and her preternatural vision.

Themes, Motifs & Symbols

Themes

Themes are the fundamental and often universal ideas explored in a literary work.

Sin, Knowledge, and the Human Condition

Sin and knowledge are linked in the Judeo-Christian tradition. The Bible begins with the story of Adam and Eve, who were expelled from the Garden of Eden for eating from the tree of knowledge of good and evil. As a result of their knowledge, Adam and Eve are made aware of their humanness, that which separates them from the divine and from other creatures. Once expelled from the Garden of Eden, they are forced to toil and to procreate—two "labors" that seem to define the human condition. The experience of Hester and Dimmesdale recalls the story of Adam and Eve because, in both cases, sin results in expulsion and suffering. But it also results in knowledge—specifically, in knowledge of what it means to be human. For Hester, the scarlet letter functions as "her passport into regions where other women dared not tread," leading her to "speculate" about her society and herself more "boldly" than anyone else in New England. As for Dimmesdale, the "burden" of his sin gives him "sympathies so intimate with the sinful brotherhood of mankind, so that his heart vibrate[s] in unison with theirs." His eloquent and powerful sermons derive from this sense of empathy. Hester and Dimmesdale contemplate their own sinfulness on a daily basis and try to reconcile it with their lived experiences. The Puritan elders, on the other hand, insist on seeing earthly experience as merely an obstacle on the path to heaven. Thus, they view sin as a threat to the community that should be punished and suppressed. Their answer to Hester's sin is to ostracize her. Yet, Puritan society is stagnant, while Hester and Dimmesdale's experience shows that a state of sinfulness can lead to personal growth, sympathy, and understanding of others. Paradoxically, these qualities are shown to be incompatible with a state of purity.

THE NATURE OF EVIL

The characters in the novel frequently debate the identity of the "Black Man," the embodiment of evil. Over the course of the novel, the "Black Man" is associated with Dimmesdale, Chillingworth, and Mistress Hibbins, and little Pearl is thought by some to be the Devil's child. The characters also try to root out the causes of evil: did Chillingworth's selfishness in marrying Hester force her to the "evil" she committed in Dimmesdale's arms? Is Hester and Dimmesdale's deed responsible for Chillingworth's transformation into a malevolent being? This confusion over the nature and causes of evil reveals the problems with the Puritan conception of sin. The book argues that true evil arises from the close relationship between hate and love. As the narrator points out in the novel's concluding chapter, both emotions depend upon "a high degree of intimacy and heart-knowledge; each renders one individual dependent . . . upon another." Evil is not found in Hester and Dimmesdale's lovemaking, nor even in the cruel ignorance of the Puritan fathers. Evil, in its most poisonous form, is found in the carefully plotted and precisely aimed revenge of Chillingworth, whose love has been perverted. Perhaps Pearl is not entirely wrong when she thinks Dimmesdale is the "Black Man," because her father, too, has perverted his love. Dimmesdale, who should love Pearl, will not even publicly acknowledge her. His cruel denial of love to his own child may be seen as further perpetrating evil.

IDENTITY AND SOCIETY

After Hester is publicly shamed and forced by the people of Boston to wear a badge of humiliation, her unwillingness to leave the town may seem puzzling. She is not physically imprisoned, and leaving the Massachusetts Bay Colony would allow her to remove the scarlet letter and resume a normal life. Surprisingly, Hester reacts with dismay when Chillingworth tells her that the town fathers are considering letting her remove the letter. Hester's behavior is premised on her desire to determine her own identity rather than to allow others to determine it for her. To her, running away or removing the letter would be an acknowledgment of society's power over her: she would be admitting that the letter is a mark of shame and something from which she desires to escape. Instead, Hester stays, refiguring the scarlet letter as a symbol of her own experiences and character. Her past sin is a part of who she is; to pretend that it never happened would mean denying a part of herself. Thus, Hester very determinedly integrates her sin into her life.

Dimmesdale also struggles against a socially determined identity. As the community's minister, he is more symbol than human being. Except for Chillingworth, those around the minister willfully ignore his obvious anguish, misinterpreting it as holiness. Unfortunately, Dimmesdale never fully recognizes the truth of what Hester has learned: that individuality and strength are gained by quiet self-assertion and by a reconfiguration, not a rejection, of one's assigned identity.

MOTIFS

Motifs are recurring structures, contrasts, and literary devices that can help to develop and inform the text's major themes.

CIVILIZATION VERSUS THE WILDERNESS
In *The Scarlet Letter,* the town and the surrounding forest represent opposing behavioral systems. The town represents civilization, a rule-bound space where everything one does is on display and where transgressions are quickly punished. The forest, on the other hand, is a space of natural rather than human authority. In the forest, society's rules do not apply, and alternate identities can be assumed. While this allows for misbehavior— Mistress Hibbins's midnight rides, for example—it also permits greater honesty and an escape from the repression of Boston. When Hester and Dimmesdale meet in the woods, for a few moments, they become happy young lovers once again. Hester's cottage, which, significantly, is located on the outskirts of town and at the edge of the forest, embodies both orders. It is her place of exile, which ties it to the authoritarian town, but because it lies apart from the settlement, it is a place where she can create for herself a life of relative peace.

NIGHT VERSUS DAY
By emphasizing the alternation between sunlight and darkness, the novel organizes the plot's events into two categories: those which are socially acceptable, and those which must take place covertly. Daylight exposes an individual's activities and makes him or her vulnerable to punishment. Night, on the other hand, conceals and enables activities that would not be possible or tolerated during the day—for instance, Dimmesdale's encounter with Hester and Pearl on the scaffold. These notions of visibility versus concealment are

linked to two of the book's larger themes—the themes of inner versus socially assigned identity and of outer appearances versus internal states. Night is the time when inner natures can manifest themselves. During the day, interiority is once again hidden from public view, and secrets remain secrets.

EVOCATIVE NAMES

The names in this novel often seem to beg to be interpreted allegorically. Chillingworth is cold and inhuman and thus brings a "chill" to Hester's and Dimmesdale's lives. "Prynne" rhymes with "sin," while "Dimmesdale" suggests "dimness"—weakness, indeterminacy, lack of insight, and lack of will, all of which characterize the young minister. The name "Pearl" evokes a biblical allegorical device—the "pearl of great price" that is salvation. This system of naming lends a profundity to the story, linking it to other allegorical works of literature such as *The Pilgrim's Progress* and to portions of the Bible. It also aligns the novel with popular forms of narrative such as fairy tales.

SYMBOLS

Symbols are objects, characters, figures, and colors used to represent abstract ideas or concepts.

THE SCARLET LETTER

The scarlet letter is meant to be a symbol of shame, but instead it becomes a powerful symbol of identity to Hester. The letter's meaning shifts as time passes. Originally intended to mark Hester as an adulterer, the "A" eventually comes to stand for "Able." Finally, it becomes indeterminate: the Native Americans who come to watch the Election Day pageant think it marks her as a person of importance and status. Like Pearl, the letter functions as a physical reminder of Hester's affair with Dimmesdale. But, compared with a human child, the letter seems insignificant, and thus helps to point out the ultimate meaninglessness of the community's system of judgment and punishment. The child has been sent from God, or at least from nature, but the letter is merely a human contrivance. Additionally, the instability of the letter's apparent meaning calls into question society's ability to use symbols for ideological reinforcement. More often than not, a symbol becomes a focal point for critical analysis and debate.

THE METEOR

As Dimmesdale stands on the scaffold with Hester and Pearl in Chapter XII, a meteor traces out an "A" in the night sky. To Dimmesdale, the meteor implies that he should wear a mark of shame just as Hester does. The meteor is interpreted differently by the rest of the community, which thinks that it stands for "Angel" and marks Governor Winthrop's entry into heaven. But "Angel" is an awkward reading of the symbol. The Puritans commonly looked to symbols to confirm divine sentiments. In this narrative, however, symbols are taken to mean what the beholder wants them to mean. The incident with the meteor obviously highlights and exemplifies two different uses of symbols: Puritan and literary.

PEARL

Although Pearl is a complex character, her primary function within the novel is as a symbol. Pearl is a sort of living version of her mother's scarlet letter. She is the physical consequence of sexual sin and the indicator of a transgression. Yet, even as a reminder of Hester's "sin," Pearl is more than a mere punishment to her mother: she is also a blessing. She represents not only "sin" but also the vital spirit and passion that engendered that sin. Thus, Pearl's existence gives her mother reason to live, bolstering her spirits when she is tempted to give up. It is only after Dimmesdale is revealed to be Pearl's father that Pearl can become fully "human." Until then, she functions in a symbolic capacity as the reminder of an unsolved mystery.

THE ROSEBUSH NEXT TO THE PRISON DOOR

The narrator chooses to begin his story with the image of the rose-bush beside the prison door. The rosebush symbolizes the ability of nature to endure and outlast man's activities. Yet, paradoxically, it also symbolizes the futility of symbolic interpretation: the narrator mentions various significances that the rosebush might have, never affirming or denying them, never privileging one over the others.

Summary & Analysis

The Custom-House: Introductory

Summary

> *A writer of story-books! What kind of a business in life,—what mode of glorifying God, or being serviceable to mankind in his day and generation,— may that be?*
>
> (See QUOTATIONS, p. 56)

This introduction provides a frame for the main narrative of *The Scarlet Letter*. The nameless narrator, who shares quite a few traits with the book's author, takes a post as the "chief executive officer," or surveyor, of the Salem Custom-House. ("Customs" are the taxes paid on foreign imports into a country; a "customhouse" is the building where these taxes are paid.) He finds the establishment to be a run-down place, situated on a rotting wharf in a half-finished building. His fellow workers mostly hold lifetime appointments secured by family connections. They are elderly and given to telling the same stories repeatedly. The narrator finds them to be generally incompetent and innocuously corrupt.

The narrator spends his days at the customhouse trying to amuse himself because few ships come to Salem anymore. One rainy day he discovers some documents in the building's unoccupied second story. Looking through the pile, he notices a manuscript that is bundled with a scarlet, gold-embroidered piece of cloth in the shape of the letter "A." The narrator examines the scarlet badge and holds it briefly to his chest, but he drops it because it seems to burn him. He then reads the manuscript. It is the work of one Jonathan Pue, who was a customs surveyor a hundred years earlier. An interest in local history led Pue to write an account of events taking place in the middle of the seventeenth century—a century before Pue's time and two hundred years before the narrator's.

The narrator has already mentioned his unease about attempting to make a career out of writing. He believes that his Puritan ancestors, whom he holds in high regard, would find it frivolous and "degenerate." Nevertheless, he decides to write a fictional account of Hester Prynne's experiences. It will not be factually precise, but he believes that it will be faithful to the spirit and general outline of the original. While working at the customhouse, surrounded by uninspiring men, the narrator finds himself unable to write. When a new president is elected, he loses his politically appointed job and, settling down before a dim fire in his parlor, begins to write his "romance," which becomes the body of *The Scarlet Letter*.

ANALYSIS

This section introduces us to the narrator and establishes his desire to contribute to American culture. Although this narrator seems to have much in common with Nathaniel Hawthorne himself— Hawthorne also worked as a customs officer, lost his job due to political changes, and had Puritan ancestors whose legacy he considered both a blessing and a curse—it is important not to conflate the two storytellers. The narrator is not just a stand-in for Hawthorne; he is carefully constructed to enhance the book aesthetically and philosophically. Moreover, Hawthorne sets him up to parallel Hester Prynne in significant ways. Like Hester, the narrator spends his days surrounded by people from whom he feels alienated. In his case, it is his relative youth and vitality that separates him from the career customs officers. Hester's youthful zest for life may have indirectly caused her alienation as well, spurring her to her sin. Similarly, like Hester, the narrator seeks out the "few who will understand him," and it is to this select group that he addresses both his own story and the tale of the scarlet letter. The narrator points out the connection between Hester and himself when he notes that he will someday be reduced to a name on a custom stamp, much as she has been reduced to a pile of old papers and a scrap of cloth. The narrator's identification with Hester enables the reader to universalize her story and to see its application to another society.

Despite his devotion to Hester's story, the narrator has trouble writing it. First, he feels that his Puritan ancestors would find it frivolous, and indeed he is not able to write until he has been relieved of any real career responsibilities. Second, he knows that his audience will be small, mostly because he is relating events that happened some two hundred years ago. His time spent in the company of the other customhouse men has taught the narrator that it will be difficult to write in such a way as to make his story accessible to all types of people—particularly to those no longer young at heart. But he regards it as part of his challenge to try to tell Hester's story in a way that makes it both meaningful and emotionally affecting to all readers. His last step in preparing to write is to stop battling the "real world" of work and small-mindedness and to give himself up to the "romance" atmosphere of his story.

The narrator finds writing therapeutic. Contrary to his Puritan ancestors' assertions, he also discovers it to be practical: his introduction provides a cogent discourse on American history and culture. Hawthorne wrote at a time when America sought to distinguish itself from centuries of European tradition by producing uniquely "American" writers—those who, like Hawthorne, would encourage patriotism by enlarging the world's sense of America's comparatively brief history.

Yet Hawthorne, like the narrator, had to balance the need to establish a weighty past with the equally compelling need to write an interesting and relevant story. Neither the narrator nor Hawthorne wants to see his work pigeonholed as "only" American. Americanness remains both a promise and a threat, just as the eagle over the customhouse door both offers shelter and appears ready to attack. The tale of the scarlet letter may add to the legitimacy of American history and culture, but in order to do so it must transcend its Americanness and establish a universal appeal: only then can American culture hold its own in the world.

Hester's story comes to us twice removed. It is filtered first through John Pue and then through the narrator. Awareness of the story's various stages of treatment gives the reader a greater sense of its remoteness from contemporary life, of its antique qualities—it is a history with a history. Yet the story's survival over the years speaks to the profundity of its themes: the narrator has found, in American history and in Hester's life, a tale rich in philosophical meaning.

CHAPTERS I–II

SUMMARY—CHAPTER I: THE PRISON-DOOR

This first chapter contains little in the way of action, instead setting the scene and introducing the first of many symbols that will come to dominate the story. A crowd of somber, dreary-looking people has gathered outside the door of a prison in seventeenth-century Boston. The building's heavy oak door is studded with iron spikes, and the prison appears to have been constructed to hold dangerous criminals. No matter how optimistic the founders of new colonies may be, the narrator tells us, they invariably provide for a prison and a cemetery almost immediately. This is true of the citizens of Boston, who built their prison some twenty years earlier.

The one incongruity in the otherwise drab scene is the rosebush that grows next to the prison door. The narrator suggests that it offers a reminder of Nature's kindness to the condemned; for his tale, he says, it will provide either a "sweet moral blossom" or else some relief in the face of unrelenting sorrow and gloom.

SUMMARY — CHAPTER II: THE MARKET-PLACE

As the crowd watches, Hester Prynne, a young woman holding an infant, emerges from the prison door and makes her way to a scaffold (a raised platform), where she is to be publicly condemned. The women in the crowd make disparaging comments about Hester; they particularly criticize her for the ornateness of the embroidered badge on her chest—a letter "A" stitched in gold and scarlet. From the women's conversation and Hester's reminiscences as she walks through the crowd, we can deduce that she has committed adultery and has borne an illegitimate child, and that the "A" on her dress stands for "Adulterer."

The beadle calls Hester forth. Children taunt her and adults stare. Scenes from Hester's earlier life flash through her mind: she sees her parents standing before their home in rural England, then she sees a "misshapen" scholar, much older than herself, whom she married and followed to continental Europe. But now the present floods in upon her, and she inadvertently squeezes the infant in her arms, causing it to cry out. She regards her current fate with disbelief.

ANALYSIS — CHAPTERS I–II

These chapters introduce the reader to Hester Prynne and begin to explore the theme of sin, along with its connection to knowledge and social order. The chapters' use of symbols, as well as their depiction of the political reality of Hester Prynne's world, testify to the contradictions inherent in Puritan society. This is a world that has already "fallen," that already knows sin: the colonists are quick to establish a prison and a cemetery in their "Utopia," for they know that misbehavior, evil, and death are unavoidable. This belief fits into the larger Puritan doctrine, which puts heavy emphasis on the idea of original sin—the notion that all people are born sinners because of the initial transgressions of Adam and Eve in the Garden of Eden.

But the images of the chapters—the public gatherings at the prison and at the scaffold, both of which are located in central common spaces—also speak to another Puritan belief: the belief that sin not only permeates our world but that it should be actively sought out and exposed so that it can be punished publicly. The beadle reinforces this belief when he calls for a "blessing on the righteous Colony of the Massachusetts, where iniquity is dragged out into the sunshine." His smug self-righteousness suggests that Hester's persecution is fueled by more than the villagers' quest for virtue. While exposing sin is meant to help the sinner and provide an example for others, such exposure does more than merely protect the community. Indeed, Hester becomes a scapegoat, and the public nature of her punishment makes her an object for voyeuristic contemplation; it also gives the townspeople, particularly the women, a chance to demonstrate—or convince themselves of—their own piety by condemning her as loudly as possible. Rather than seeing their own potential sinfulness in Hester, the townspeople see her as someone whose transgressions outweigh and obliterate their own errors.

Yet, unlike her fellow townspeople, Hester accepts her humanity rather than struggles against it; in many ways, her "sin" originated in her acknowledgment of her human need for love, following her husband's unexplained failure to arrive in Boston and his probable death. The women of the town criticize her for embroidering the scarlet letter, the symbol of her shame, with such care and in such a flashy manner: its ornateness seems to declare that she is proud, rather than ashamed, of her sin. In reality, however, Hester simply accepts the "sin" and its symbol as part of herself, just as she accepts her child. And although she can hardly believe her present "realities," she takes them as they are rather than resisting them or trying to atone for them.

Both the rosebush and Hester resist the kinds of fixed interpretation that the narrator associates with religion. The narrator offers multiple possibilities for the significance of the rosebush near the prison door, as he puzzles over its survival in his source manuscript. But, in the end, he rejects all of its possible "meanings," refusing to give the rosebush a definitive interpretation.

So, too, does the figure of Hester offer various options for interpretation. The fact that she is a woman with a past, with memories of a childhood in England, a marriage in Europe, and a journey to America, means that, despite what the Puritan community thinks, she cannot be defined solely in terms of a single action, in terms of her great "sin." Pearl, her child, is evidence of this: her existence makes the scarlet letter redundant in that it is she and not the snippet of fabric that is the true consequence of Hester's actions. As Pearl matures in the coming chapters and her role in Hester's life becomes more complex, the part Hester's "sin" plays in defining her identity will become more difficult to determine. For now, the infant's presence highlights the insignificance of the community's attempt at punishment: Pearl is a sign of a larger, more powerful order than that which the community is attempting to assert—be it nature, biology, or a God untainted by the corruptions of human religious practices. The fact that the townspeople focus on the scarlet letter rather than on the human child underlines their pettiness, and their failure to see the more "real" consequences of Hester's action.

From this point forward, Hester will be formally, officially set apart from the rest of society; yet these opening chapters imply that, even before her acquisition of the scarlet letter, she had always been unique. The text describes her appearance as more distinctive than conventionally beautiful: she is tall and radiates a natural nobility that sets her apart from the women of the town, with whom she is immediately juxtaposed. Hester's physical isolation on the scaffold thus only manifests an internal alienation that predates the beginning of the plot.

This is the first of three important scenes involving the scaffold. Each of these scenes will show a character taking the first step toward a sort of Emersonian self-reliance, the kind of self-reliance that would come to replace Puritan ideology as the American ideal. In this scene, Hester confronts her "realities" and discovers a new self that does not fit with her old conceptions of herself. Puritan doctrine views "reality" as merely an obstacle to a world beyond this one; Hester's need to embrace her current situation (in part by literally embracing her daughter) implies a profound separation from the ideals of that ideological system. From now on, Hester will stand outside, if still surrounded by, the Puritan order.

CHAPTERS III–IV

SUMMARY—CHAPTER III: THE RECOGNITION

In the crowd that surrounds the scaffold, Hester suddenly spots her husband, who sent her to America but never fulfilled his promise to follow her. Though he is dressed in a strange combination of traditional European clothing and Native American dress, she is struck by his wise countenance and recognizes his slightly deformed shoulders. Hester's husband (whom we will learn, in the next chapters, is now calling himself Roger Chillingworth) gestures to Hester that she should not reveal his identity. He then turns to a stranger in the crowd and asks about Hester's crime and punishment, explaining that he has been held captive by Native Americans and has just arrived in Boston. The stranger tells him that Hester is the wife of a learned Englishman and had been living with him in Amsterdam when he decided to emigrate to America. The learned man sent Hester to America first and remained behind to settle his affairs, but he never joined Hester in Boston. Chillingworth remarks that Hester's husband must have been foolish to think he could keep a young wife happy, and he asks the stranger about the identity of the baby's father.

The stranger tells him that Hester refuses to reveal her fellow sinner. As punishment, she has been sentenced to three hours on the scaffold and a lifetime of wearing the scarlet letter on her chest. The narrator then introduces us to the town fathers who sit in judgment of Hester: Governor Bellingham, Reverend Wilson, and Reverend Dimmesdale. Dimmesdale, a young minister who is renowned for his eloquence, religious fervor, and theological expertise, is delegated to demand that Hester reveal the name of her child's father. He tells her that she should not protect the man's identity out of pity or tenderness, but when she staunchly refuses he does not press her further. Hester says that her child will seek a heavenly father and will never know an earthly one. Reverend Wilson then steps in and delivers a condemnatory sermon on sin, frequently referring to Hester's scarlet letter, which seems to the crowd to glow and burn. Hester bears the sermon patiently, hushing Pearl when she begins to scream. At the conclusion of the sermon, Hester is led back into the prison.

SUMMARY—CHAPTER IV: THE INTERVIEW

Hester and her husband come face to face for the first time when he is called to her prison cell to provide medical assistance. Chillingworth has promised the jailer that he can make Hester more "amenable to just authority," and he now offers her a cup of medicine. Hester knows his true identity—his gaze makes her shudder—and she initially refuses to drink his potion. She thinks that Chillingworth might be poisoning her, but he assures her that he wants her to live so that he can have his revenge. In the candid conversation that follows, he chastises himself for thinking that he, a misshapen bookworm, could keep a beautiful wife like Hester happy. He urges her to reveal the identity of her lover, telling her that he will surely detect signs of sympathy that will lead him to the guilty party. When she refuses to tell her secret, he makes her promise that she will not reveal to anyone his own identity either. His demoniacal grin and obvious delight at her current tribulations lead Hester to burst out the speculation that he may be the "Black Man"—the Devil in disguise—come to lure her into a pact and damn her soul. Chillingworth replies that it is not the well-being of her soul that his presence jeopardizes, implying that he plans to seek out her unknown lover. He clearly has revenge on his mind.

ANALYSIS — CHAPTERS III–IV

The town has made Hester into a "living sermon," as Chillingworth puts it, because she is stripped of her humanity and made to serve the needs of the community. Her punishment is expressed in violent terms. Reverend Wilson relates an argument he had with Dimmesdale about whether to force Hester to confess in public. Dimmesdale spoke of such an action in terms of a rape, arguing that "it were wronging the very nature of woman to force her to lay open her heart's secrets in such broad daylight, and in presence of so great a multitude."

The men who sit in judgment of Hester are not only hypocritical but also ignorant. Bellingham, surrounded by the trappings of his office, and Wilson, who looks like "the darkly engraved portraits which we see prefixed to old volumes of sermons," both occupy positions where power is dependent upon self-portrayal and symbols. They know little of human nature and judge using overarching precepts rather than the specifics of an individual situation as their guides. The narrator tells us that these ignorant men "had no right" to "meddle with a question of human guilt, passion and anguish." Dimmesdale, on the other hand, seems to know something of the human heart. He is compassionate toward Hester and is able to convince Bellingham and Wilson to spare her any harsher punishment.

As part of its meditation on the concept of evil, the text begins to elucidate Dimmesdale's character for the reader. The emerging portrait is not altogether positive. Although Dimmesdale displays compassion and a sense of justice, he also seems spineless and somewhat sinister. His efforts to get Hester to reveal her lover's identity involve a set of confusing instructions about following her conscience and exposing her lover in order to save his soul. The reader does not know why Dimmesdale declines to speak straightforwardly, but Hester does. When it is later revealed that Dimmesdale is the lover she seeks to protect, his speech becomes retrospectively ironic and terribly cruel. In this way, *The Scarlet Letter* comes to resemble a detective story: things have meaning only in the context of later information. The larger implication of such a structure is that lives have meaning only as a whole, and that an individual event (Hester's adultery, for example) must be examined in a framework larger than that allowed by the categorical rules of religion. This notion returns the reader to the book's general theme of whether it is ethically right to judge others.

Chillingworth, too, begins to come into focus in these pages. The novel sets up a formal parallel between Dimmesdale and Chillingworth before the story makes clear the logical connection between the two characters. In contrast to Wilson's dehumanizing condemnations and to Dimmesdale's mysterious circuitousness, Chillingworth's willingness to take some of the blame for Hester's "fall" seems almost noble. He admits that he was not the right husband for Hester and that he was remiss in not joining up with her sooner (even though he seems to have been held captive). Yet, he ultimately chooses to use his knowledge for vengeance. While he is less hypocritical than the Puritan fathers, who claim to want only the salvation of their followers, Chillingworth, as the name he takes suggests, is devoid of human warmth. His marriage to Hester—his one attempt at human contact—has led to disaster, and any compassion he may once have felt has now faded. Bellingham, Wilson, and the rest of the Puritan leadership come across as bumbling, ignorant, and silly in their pageantry and ritual when compared with the intentionally malevolent Chillingworth, who seeks revenge, destruction, and sin. Perhaps most cunningly, he forces Hester to become the keeper of everyone's secrets, thus stripping her of any chance she may have had at redemption or a happy life. Chillingworth's physical deformity mirrors his spiritual deformity. As Hester suggests, he is like the "Black Man," because he lures others into sin. By emphasizing Chillingworth's scholarly training, the text puts a spin on the biblical equation of knowledge with evil: here it is knowledge without compassion or human experience that is the greatest evil.

Chapters V–VI

Summary—Chapter V: Hester at Her Needle

The narrator covers the events of several years. After a few months, Hester is released from prison. Although she is free to leave Boston, she chooses not to do so. She settles in an abandoned cabin on a patch of infertile land at the edge of town. Hester remains alienated from everyone, including the town fathers, respected women, beggars, children, and even strangers. She serves as a walking example of a fallen woman, a cautionary tale for everyone to see. Although she is an outcast, Hester remains able to support herself due to her uncommon talent in needlework. Her taste for the beautiful infuses her embroidery, rendering her work fit to be worn by the governor despite its shameful source. Although the ornate detail of her artistry defies Puritan codes of fashion, it is in demand for burial shrouds, christening gowns, and officials' robes. In fact, through her work, Hester touches all the major events of life except for marriage—it is deemed inappropriate for chaste brides to wear the product of Hester Prynne's hands. Despite her success, Hester feels lonely and is constantly aware of her alienation. As shame burns inside of her, she searches for companionship or sympathy, but to no avail. She devotes part of her time to charity work, but even this is more punishment than solace: those she helps frequently insult her, and making garments for the poor out of rough cloth insults her aesthetic sense.

Summary—Chapter VI: Pearl

Hester's one consolation is her daughter, Pearl, who is described in great detail in this chapter. A beautiful flower growing out of sinful soil, Pearl is so named because she was "purchased with all [Hester] had—her mother's only treasure!" Because "in giving her existence a great law had been broken," Pearl's very being seems to be inherently at odds with the strict rules of Puritan society. Pearl has inherited all of Hester's moodiness, passion, and defiance, and she constantly makes mischief. Hester loves but worries about her child.

When the narrator describes Pearl as an "outcast," he understates: Pearl is an "imp of evil, emblem and product of sin, she had no right among christened infants." Pearl herself is aware of her difference from others, and when Hester tries to teach her about God, Pearl says, "I have no Heavenly Father!" Because Pearl is her mother's constant companion, she, too, is subject to the cruelties of the townspeople. The other children are particularly cruel because they can sense that something is not quite right about Hester and her child. Knowing that she is alone in this world, Pearl creates casts of characters in her imagination to keep her company.

Pearl is fascinated by the scarlet letter and at times seems to intentionally torture her mother by playing with it. Once, when Pearl is pelting the letter with wildflowers, Hester exclaims in frustration, "Child, what art thou?" Pearl turns the question back on her mother, insisting that Hester tell her of her origins. Surprised at the impudence of a child so young (Pearl is about three at the time), Hester wonders if Pearl might not be the demon-child that many of the townspeople believe her to be.

ANALYSIS—CHAPTERS V–VI

Chapter V deals with one of the primary questions of the book: why does Hester choose to stay in Boston when she is free to leave? The narrator offers several explanations. Hester's explanation to herself is that New England was the scene of her crime; therefore, it should also be the scene of her punishment. The narrator adds that Hester's life has been too deeply marked by the things that have happened to her here for her to leave. Additionally, he adds, Hester feels bound to Pearl's father, who presumably continues to live in Boston. But there seems to be more to Hester's refusal to leave. Were she to escape to Europe or into the wilderness, Hester would be acknowledging society's power over the course of her life. By staying and facing cruel taunts and alienation, Hester insists, paradoxically, upon her right to self-determination. Hester does not need to flee or to live a life of lies in order to resist the judgment against her.

Each time she interacts with Pearl, Hester is forced to reconsider the life she has chosen for herself. Pearl is both the sign of Hester's shame and her greatest treasure—she is a punishment and a consolation. Pearl reminds Hester of her transgression, of the act that has left Hester in her current state of alienation. And Pearl's ostracism by the community recalls Hester's own feelings of exile. Yet, Pearl's existence also suggests that out of sin comes treasure. This idea is reinforced by Hester's needlework: out of necessity born of shame, luxury and beauty are crafted.

It is fitting that Pearl is fascinated by the scarlet letter, as the child and the emblem are read similarly by society. Like Pearl, the letter inspires a mixture of contempt and strange enchantment. Both also invite contemplation: people—even the narrator, some two hundred years later—feel compelled to tell the story behind the two relics.

The children of the townspeople are as cruel as their parents in their treatment of Hester and Pearl. In their "play," the underlying attitudes of the community are revealed. The Puritans-in-training make believe they are scalping Native Americans, they mimic the gestures of going to church, and they pretend to engage in witch-craft. They mirror the true preoccupations of their parents, just as Pearl reflects the complex state of her exiled mother. Indeed, Hester frequently uses Pearl as a mirror, watching her own reflection in the child's eyes.

It is in these chapters that the book's romance atmosphere emerges. (The term "romance" here refers to an emphasis on the supernatural, the unrealistic, or the magical in order to explore alternatives to the "reality" of human existence.) Hester's cottage on the edge of the forest functions as a space where the mores of the town do not wield as much authority. As we will see later, the forest itself represents even greater freedom. Pearl seems to be a kind of changeling—a surreal, elfin creature who challenges reality and thrives on fantasy and strangeness. This world of near-magic is, of course, utterly un-Puritan. At times it seems almost un-human. Yet the genius of Hawthorne's technique here is that he uses the "un-human" elements of Hester and Pearl's life together to empha-size their very humanness. The text suggests that being fully human means not denying one's human nature. By indulging in dream, imagination, beauty, and passion, one accesses a world that is more magically transcendent.

CHAPTERS VII–VIII

SUMMARY—CHAPTER VII: THE GOVERNOR'S HALL

Hester pays a visit to Governor Bellingham's mansion. She has two intentions: to deliver a pair of ornate gloves she has made for the governor, and to find out if there is any truth to the rumors that Pearl, now three, may be taken from her. Some of the townspeople, apparently including the governor, have come to suspect Pearl of being a sort of demon-child. The townspeople reason that if Pearl is a demon-child, she should be taken from Hester for Hester's sake. And, they reason, if Pearl is indeed a human child, she should be taken away from her mother for her own sake and given to a "bet-ter" parent than Hester Prynne. On their way to see the governor,

Hester and Pearl are attacked by a group of children, who try to fling mud at them. Pearl becomes angry and frightens the children off.

The governor's mansion is stuffy and severe. It is built in the style of the English aristocracy, complete with family portraits and a suit of armor, which the governor has worn in battles with the Native Americans. Pearl is fascinated by the armor. When she points out her mother's reflection in it, Hester is horrified to see that the scarlet letter dominates the reflection. Pearl begins to scream for a rose from the bush outside the window, but she is quieted by the entrance of a group of men.

SUMMARY — CHAPTER VIII:
THE ELF-CHILD AND THE MINISTER

Bellingham, Wilson, Chillingworth, and Dimmesdale enter the room. They notice Pearl and begin to tease her by calling her a bird and a demon-child. When the governor points out that Hester is also present, they ask her why she should be allowed to keep the child. She tells the men that she will be able to teach Pearl an important lesson—the lesson that she has learned from her shame. They are doubtful, and Wilson tries to test the three-year-old's knowledge of religious subjects. Wilson resents Pearl's seeming dislike of him, and Pearl's refusal to answer even the simplest of questions does not bode well.

With nowhere else to turn, Hester begs Dimmesdale to speak for her and her child. He replies by reminding the men that God sent Pearl and that the child was seemingly meant to be both a blessing and a curse. Swayed by his eloquence, Bellingham and Wilson agree not to separate mother and child. Strangely, Pearl has taken well to Dimmesdale. She goes to him and presses his hand to her cheek. Vexed because Hester seems to have triumphed, Chillingworth presses the men to reopen their investigation into the identity of Hester's lover, but they refuse, telling him that God will reveal the information when He deems it appropriate. As Hester leaves the governor's mansion, Mistress Hibbins, the governor's sister, pokes her head out of the window to invite Hester to a witches' gathering. Hester tells her that if she had not been able to keep Pearl, she would have gone willingly. The narrator notes that it seems Pearl has saved her mother from Satan's temptations.

ANALYSIS—CHAPTERS VII–VIII

These chapters link Pearl even more explicitly to the scarlet letter. Hester dresses her daughter in "a crimson velvet tunic of a peculiar cut, abundantly embroidered with fantasies and flourishes of gold thread." Pearl and the embroidered letter are both beautiful in a rich, sensuous way that stands in contrast to the stiffness of Puritan society. Indeed, the narrator explicitly tells the reader that Pearl is "the scarlet letter endowed with life." The narrator tells us that Hester has worked to create an "analogy between the object of [Hester's] affection and the emblem of her guilt and torture." This reinforces the contradictory nature of both the letter and Pearl, for just as Hester both loves and feels burdened by Pearl, her thoughts regarding the scarlet letter seem also to contain a touch of fondness. Certainly her attitude toward it is not one of uniform regret, and she may even harbor pleasant associations with the deeds that the letter symbolizes. The sin itself was both a guilty act and an act of affection, a problematic combination of love and "evil."

The letter and the child also hold a dual meaning for the town fathers. They understand that both child and badge function as reminders of sin and as protections against further sin. Dimmesdale momentarily acknowledges this in his speech, but the purpose of his words is not to ponder ambiguities but rather to point to these ambiguities as proof of the futility of all interpretation. Pearl, he says, came from God, and therefore must be intended as Hester's companion. According to Dimmesdale, any attempt to interpret her presence otherwise would be in vain because no one has knowledge of God's intentions.

Governor Bellingham's mansion is rich in symbolic detail. The narrator tells us that it replicates an English nobleman's home, and Bellingham proudly displays his ancestors' portraits. Puritans certainly didn't seek to reject English culture as a whole, but it is nevertheless important that Bellingham has chosen to re-create a piece of the old world in the new. Bellingham's ties to the world that the Puritans supposedly left behind suggest that he has brought with him the very things the Puritans sought to escape by leaving England: intolerance and a lack of freedom. The state of the governor's garden implies that such translations of old into new may not be as seamless as the governor wishes. The garden, planted in the English ornamental style, is in a state of decay. The decorative plants have not taken root, and the garden's creator appears to have given up.

Cabbages, pumpkins, and a few rosebushes are all that has grown there. The English ornamental plants serve as symbols of the principles and ideals of the old world, which cannot be successfully transplanted to America.

The decaying garden can also be read in other ways. Its need of maintenance suggests that Bellingham is not capable of nurturing things—including the society he is supposed to govern. The fertility of the cabbages and the pumpkins hints at the fundamental incompatibility of ideals with the necessities of life. The garden was intended to provide a pleasing aesthetic experience, but it ends up serving only a practical purpose by growing food. The one aesthetic object that does grow in the garden is a rosebush, which explicitly links ideals to pain—every rose, after all, has its thorn.

The governor's suit of armor is another meaningful item. It is suggestive of war and violence, but while describing the armor, the narrator takes the opportunity to mention that Bellingham trained as a lawyer. In the same way that war requires soldiers to leave their jobs and fight for their country, the "exigencies of this new country" led Bellingham to take on the roles of statesman and soldier. Such a comparison suggests that Bellingham may be incompetent in his newly adopted careers, or at least that he has overextended himself. The armor also functions as a distorting mirror, and Hester's out-of-scale reflection signifies her unnatural place in society.

The final paradox of the governor's house is Mistress Hibbins, the acknowledged witch who is Governor Bellingham's sister. Something is clearly awry in a society that allows a woman who admittedly engages in satanic practices to remain a protected and acknowledged member of the community, while it forces Hester, who has erred but once, to live as an outcast and in danger of losing her child.

It is Pearl who points out many of these disturbing and significant images. In these scenes, she shows herself to be not only a spiritual help to her mother but also a kind of oracle of truth. Accurately sensing the sinister aura of the place, she tries to escape out a window. Most important, she shuns Wilson and clings to Dimmesdale, exhibiting what we will later understand as a profound subconscious insight: her instinct leads her away from the representative of her "heavenly father" and toward her true, "earthly" father. Her impulse also reflects on the relative characters of the two men. Wilson, as she senses, is not to be trusted, while Dimmesdale, although he refuses to acknowledge his guilt, will ultimately remain loyal to her and her mother.

CHAPTERS IX–X

SUMMARY — CHAPTER IX: THE LEECH

By renaming himself upon his arrival in Boston, Chillingworth has hidden his past from everyone except Hester, whom he has sworn to secrecy. He incorporates himself into society in the role of a doctor, and since the townsfolk have very little access to good medical care, he is welcomed and valued. In addition to his training in European science, he also has some knowledge of "native" or "natural" remedies, because he was captured by Native Americans and lived with them for a time. The town sometimes refers to the doctor colloquially as a "leech," which was a common epithet for physicians at the time. The name derives from the practice of using leeches to drain blood from their patients, which used to be regarded as a curative process.

Much to the community's concern, Dimmesdale has been suffering from severe health problems. He appears to be wasting away, and he frequently clutches at his chest as though his heart pains him. Because Dimmesdale refuses to marry any of the young women who have devoted themselves to him, Chillingworth urges the town leadership to insist that Dimmesdale allow the doctor to live with him. In this way, Chillingworth may have a chance to diagnose and cure the younger man. The two men take rooms next to the cemetery in a widow's home, which gives them an opportunity for the contemplation of sin and death. The minister's room is hung with tapestries depicting biblical scenes of adultery and its punishment, while Chillingworth's room contains a laboratory that is sophisticated for its time.

The townspeople were initially grateful for Chillingworth's presence and deemed his arrival a divine miracle designed to help Dimmesdale. As time has passed, however, rumors have spread concerning Chillingworth's personal history. Even more ominously, the man's face has begun to take on a look of evil. A majority of the townspeople begin to suspect that Chillingworth is the Devil, come to wage battle for Dimmesdale's soul.

SUMMARY — CHAPTER X: THE LEECH AND HIS PATIENT

The inwardly tortured minister soon becomes Chillingworth's greatest puzzle. The doctor relentlessly and mercilessly seeks to find the root of his patient's condition. Chillingworth shows great persistence in inquiring into the most private details of Dimmesdale's life, but Dimmesdale has grown suspicious of all men and will confide in no one. Chillingworth devotes all of his time to his patient. Even when he is not in Dimmesdale's presence, Chillingworth is busy gathering herbs and weeds out of which to make medicines.

One day Dimmesdale questions his doctor about an unusual-looking plant. Chillingworth remarks that he found it growing on an unmarked grave and suggests that the dark weeds are the sign of the buried person's unconfessed sin. The two enter into an uncomfortable conversation about confession, redemption, and the notion of "burying" one's secrets. As they speak, they hear a cry from outside. Through the window, they see Pearl dancing in the graveyard and hooking burrs onto the "A" on Hester's chest. When Pearl notices the two men, she drags her mother away, saying that the "Black Man" has already gotten the minister and that he must not capture them too. Chillingworth remarks that Hester is not a woman who lives with buried sin—she wears her sin openly on her breast. At Chillingworth's words, Dimmesdale is careful not to give himself away either as someone who is intimately attached to Hester or as someone with a "buried" sin of his own. Chillingworth begins to prod the minister more directly by inquiring about his spiritual condition, explaining that he thinks it relevant to his physical health. Dimmesdale becomes agitated and tells Chillingworth that such matters are the concern of God. He then leaves the room.

Dimmesdale's behavior has reinforced Chillingworth's suspicions. The minister apologizes for his behavior, and the two are friends again. However, a few days later, Chillingworth sneaks up to Dimmesdale while he is asleep and pushes aside the shirt that Dimmesdale is wearing. What he sees on Dimmesdale's chest causes the doctor to rejoice, but the reader is kept in the dark as to what Chillingworth has found there.

ANALYSIS—CHAPTERS IX–X

These chapters explore the relationship between Chillingworth and Dimmesdale. On one level, Chillingworth represents "science" and Dimmesdale represents "spirituality." Though both of these systems offer resources to restore a person's well-being, neither seems to cure Dimmesdale's affliction. Like Chillingworth's deformed shoulders, Dimmesdale's illness is an outward manifestation of an inward condition, and neither medicine nor religion suffices to cure it. What hampers his recovery is his inability to confess his adultery with Hester, which seems to be due, at least in part, to the community's dependence on the young minister. He understands that he, like Hester, is a symbol of something larger than himself—in his case, piety and goodness. In a way, confessing would mean healing himself at the expense of the community.

Dimmesdale ponders other, seemingly irreconcilable moral considerations. The many contradictions that he encounters may stem from the constrictive and sometimes hypocritical nature of the moral system. For example, the minister refuses to marry any of the women in the community who show concern for him, both out of a sense of commitment to Hester and out of an unwillingness to implicate an innocent third party in a dark history of "sin." On the other hand, by passively waiting for God to sort things out, as he declares himself to be doing, Dimmesdale causes Hester to suffer terribly.

Yet, medicine, too, proves an inadequate solution to Dimmesdale's dilemma, as it ignores the connection between the physical and the spiritual. Chillingworth sees this, and in his practice he tries to bridge the divide, but in the most perverse of ways. It is no accident that Chillingworth is called a "leech," for he has attached himself to the minister's side like an insidiously destructive worm. He wants to use his scientific knowledge to get "deep into his patient's bosom, delving among his principles, prying into his recollections, and probing everything with a cautious touch, like a treasure-seeker in a dark cavern." Having harbored suspicion from the start, the doctor now undertakes a series of controlled experiments. His references to Hester and to buried sin are designed to remind Dimmesdale of his guilt. When Chillingworth first visited Hester in her prison cell, she asked him whether he was the Devil come to vie for her soul, and he answered that it was another's soul that would be the true focus of his malevolence. He now fulfills this evil promise: even the townspeople now regard him as the Devil come to tempt and torment their virtuous reverend.

Covertly tortured by the doctor, Dimmesdale searches for something to soothe his suffering. He envies those who can display their agonies publicly. Thus, when Chillingworth asks, "Is Hester Prynne the less miserable, think you, for that scarlet letter on her breast?" Dimmesdale answers, "I do verily believe it." He believes that the acute pain of his private suffering is far worse: "It must needs be better," he says, "for the sufferer to be free to show his pain, as this poor woman Hester is, than to cover it all up in his heart." Hester can literally wear her pain on her chest, while Dimmesdale's pain remains locked inside his body. And Dimmesdale can never atone, because he can never confess. While Hester feels shame because of the community's disapproval of her, Dimmesdale suffers from guilt, which is the product of an internalized self-disapproval and thus is much more toxic.

Pearl's character in these chapters stands in radical—and damning—contrast to the characters of both men. Whereas the men represent authority (Dimmesdale the authority of the church, Chillingworth that of accumulated knowledge), Pearl has no respect for external authority and holds nothing sacred. Similarly, whereas the two men deeply respect their forebears, Pearl has no such respect for inherited history. Chillingworth says, frowning, that the child lacks a reverence for "human ordinances or opinions, right or wrong," and for established social rules. Dimmesdale, too, says that he can discern no unified principle in Pearl's being, "save the freedom of a broken law."

Yet Pearl is not merely a negative figure; she is also a positive element, because she illuminates truths and seeks to open closed minds. Pearl's reactions to her mother's scarlet letter reveal this aspect of her. When Pearl covers the letter with burrs, she literalizes Hester's experience of living with the letter: the badge of dishonor digs painfully into Hester's being. As an innocent child, free from the strictures of organized systems, Pearl is able to discern and understand a more complex version of human experience than can either of the two much older and allegedly "wiser" men.

Chillingworth's glimpse at Dimmesdale's bared chest brings these chapters to a climax. From the enormous glee that Chillingworth shows, we may infer that he has found what he considers to be proof of the reverend's guilt—perhaps the reverend bears some form of an "A"-shaped mark upon his own skin. For now, the spectacle on the minister's chest seems to serve as a reminder of the futility of human endeavors. No matter how conniving Chillingworth's machinations, they could never have led him to a conclusion as definitive as this sighting has been. As though it were a sign from some supernatural power, Chillingworth views the sleeping minister's breast with "wonder."

Chapters XI–XII

Summary—Chapter XI: The Interior of a Heart
Chillingworth continues to play mind games with Dimmesdale, making his revenge as terrible as possible. The minister often regards

his doctor with distrust and even loathing, but because he can assign no rational basis to his feelings, he dismisses them and continues to suffer. Dimmesdale's suffering, however, does inspire him to deliver some of his most powerful sermons, which focus on the topic of sin. His struggles allow him to empathize with human weakness, and he thus addresses "the whole human brotherhood in the heart's native language." Although the reverend deeply yearns to confess the truth of his sin to his parishioners, he cannot bring himself to do so. As a result, his self-probing keeps him up at night, and he even sees visions.

In one vision, he sees Hester and "little Pearl in her scarlet garb." Hester points "her forefinger, first at the scarlet letter on her bosom, and then at the clergyman's own breast." The minister understands that he is delusional, but his psychological tumult leads him to assign great meaning to his delusions. Even the Bible offers him little support. Unable to unburden himself of the guilt deriving from his sin, he begins to believe that "the whole universe is false, . . . it shrinks to nothing within his grasp." Dimmesdale begins to torture himself physically: he scourges himself with a whip, he fasts, and he holds extended vigils, during which he stays awake throughout the night meditating upon his sin. During one of these vigils, Dimmesdale seizes on an idea for what he believes may be a remedy to his pain. He decides to hold a vigil on the scaffold where, years before, Hester suffered for her sin.

SUMMARY — CHAPTER XII: THE MINISTER'S VIGIL
Dimmesdale mounts the scaffold. The pain in his breast causes him to scream aloud, and he worries that everyone in the town will wake up and come to look at him. Fortunately for Dimmesdale, the few townspeople who heard the cry took it for a witch's voice. As Dimmesdale stands upon the scaffold, his mind turns to absurd thoughts. He almost laughs when he sees Reverend Wilson, and in his delirium he thinks that he calls out to the older minister. But Wilson, coming from the deathbed of Governor Winthrop (the colony's first governor), passes without noticing the penitent. Having come so close to being sighted, Dimmesdale begins to fantasize about what would happen if everyone in town were to witness their holy minister standing in the place of public shame.

Dimmesdale laughs aloud and is answered by a laugh from Pearl, whose presence he had not noticed. Hester and Pearl had also been at Winthrop's deathbed because the talented seamstress had been asked to make the governor's burial robe. Dimmesdale invites them to join him on the scaffold, which they do. The three hold hands, forming an "electric chain." The minister feels energized and warmed by their presence. Pearl innocently asks, "Wilt thou stand here with Mother and me, tomorrow noontide?" but the minister replies, "Not now, child, but at another time." When she presses him to name that time, he answers, "At the great judgment day."

Suddenly, a meteor brightens the dark sky, momentarily illuminating their surroundings. When the minister looks up, he sees an "A" in the sky, marked out in dull red light. At the same time, Pearl points to a figure that stands in the distance and watches them. It is Chillingworth. Dimmesdale asks Hester who Chillingworth really is, because the man occasions in him what he calls "a nameless horror." But Hester, sworn to secrecy, cannot reveal her husband's identity. Pearl says that she knows, but when she speaks into the minister's ear, she pronounces mere childish gibberish. Dimmesdale asks if she intends to mock him, and she replies that she is punishing him for his refusal to stand in public with her and her mother.

Chillingworth approaches and coaxes Dimmesdale down, saying that the minister must have sleepwalked his way up onto the scaffold. When Dimmesdale asks how Chillingworth knew where to find him, Chillingworth says that he, too, was making his way home from Winthrop's deathbed.

Dimmesdale and Chillingworth return home. The following day, the minister preaches his most powerful sermon to date. After the sermon, the church sexton hands Dimmesdale a black glove that was found on the scaffold. The sexton recognized it as the minister's, but concluded only that Satan must have been up to some mischief. The sexton then reveals another startling piece of information: he says that there has been report of a meteor falling last night in the shape of a letter "A." The townspeople have interpreted it as having nothing to do with either Hester or Dimmesdale. Rather, they believe it to stand for "Angel" and take it as a sign that Governor Winthrop has ascended to heaven.

ANALYSIS — CHAPTERS XI–XII

These chapters mark the apex of Dimmesdale's spiritual and moral crisis. Dimmesdale has tried to invent for himself an alternate path to absolution, torturing himself both psychologically and physically. The nearly hysterical fear he feels when he imagines his congregation seeing him on the scaffold is a reminder that the minister has not only himself but also his flock to consider. His public disgrace could harden his followers, or even lead them astray. However, the events in these chapters suggest that Dimmesdale must publicly confront the truth about his past. He has a strong impulse to confess to his congregation, and, although he resists it, his attempts at private expiation begin to bring him closer to exposure.

The scaffold is an important symbol of the difference between Hester's and Dimmesdale's situations. It helps to establish an ironic contrast between her public torments and his inner anguish. Dimmesdale's meeting with Hester and Pearl atop the scaffold echoes Hester's public shaming seven years earlier. This time, however, no audience bears witness to the minister's confession of sin. In fact, it is so dark outside that he is not even visible to Reverend Wilson when the latter walks past.

When Dimmesdale refuses Pearl's request that he stand with her on the scaffold in broad daylight, she refuses to share what she knows about Chillingworth. Pearl thus makes a statement about the causal connection between Dimmesdale's denial of his own guilt and his incomplete understanding of the world around him. As long as he hides the truth about himself, he can never discover the truths of others. Increasingly, Dimmesdale's hallucinations seem more real than his daily encounters. His visions never wholly delude him, however, and he remains painfully aware of his reliance upon fictions.

The Puritan world of *The Scarlet Letter* survives through convenient fictions. In the communal mind of the townspeople, Hester is the epitome of sinfulness, the minister is the embodiment of piety, and Mistress Hibbins is the governor's sister and thus cannot possibly be a witch, despite all clues to the contrary. Within this reductive system of thought, everyone fits into a category that enables him or her to be read as an illustrative example that reinforces a coherent order.

Yet, unlike his society, Dimmesdale recognizes that such categorizations can be fictions. In fact, it is his acute awareness of the dichotomy between his public image and his private self that leads him to new levels of insight, enabling his preaching to become ever more powerful and persuasive. Dimmesdale can speak of the ravages of sin because he lives them. He brings to his sermons sympathy for others and a strong sense of the daily terror to which a sinful life can lead. He understands that the worst consequence of sin is, practically speaking, separation from one's fellow man, not separation from God. This more complicated definition of sin is one of the important themes of the novel.

Curiously, while Dimmesdale sees the dangers of formulaic reductions and distortions of reality, he does little to overturn them—either those he himself lives by or those upheld by his community. Much of his daily misery is caused by the willingness of those around him to play God, to stand in judgment, and, in the case of Chillingworth, to mete out punishment.

Although none of the characters explicitly challenges the Puritan order, several events within these chapters do offer an implicit rebuke. The structural juxtaposition of Governor Winthrop's death with Dimmesdale's crisis is significant. Winthrop was one of the founders of the Massachusetts Bay Colony and its first governor. As one of the men responsible for the beginning of Puritan society, he would naturally have had to insist upon a strict adherence to Puritan ideals. His death signals the passing of an older order and suggests that the Massachusetts colony has existed long enough that a strict and literal observance of the rules is no longer necessary to ensure the colony's survival. Perhaps someone like Hester no longer constitutes a threat to social stability in this no longer new—and thus no longer as fragile—community; perhaps the policing of others is no longer critical to the colony's well-being.

Winthrop's death and Dimmesdale's guilt are jointly marked by the meteor's "A"-shaped path. To faithful Puritans, signs, particularly natural ones, were of the utmost importance, and were read as symbols of divine will. Unlike those found in most literature, symbols in the Puritan sense do not signify in complicated or contradictory ways. Instead, they tend to serve, particularly for the characters in this novel, as reinforcements of things that are already "known." The narrator makes a point of this by often juxtaposing his own, literary interpretations of signs—which tend to be more philosophical or metaphorical—with the Puritan community's more "confident" or "concrete" interpretations. Here, as the narrator recognizes, the meteor physically and figuratively illuminates Dimmesdale, Hester, and Pearl, and it exposes their relationship to Chillingworth. Yet the Puritan characters see the event as definitive "proof" of their governor's ascent to heaven. While the characters' more fixed symbolic interpretations provide the reader with little insight into the true nature of the celestial "A," they nevertheless speak volumes about the minds from which they spring. Thus Dimmesdale reads the "A" in the sky as his own, divinely sent scarlet letter. His constant burden of guilt taints and controls the way he sees the world. So, too, does the community's reading of the "A" as standing for "Angel" testify to its mindset. The townspeople see only what they want to see, a tendency that is reaffirmed the following morning when the sexton invents a story to prevent the discovery of Dimmesdale's glove from seeming suspicious.

As we will see, the deliberate rereading of Hester's scarlet letter that takes place in the following chapters will, like Dimmesdale's glove, bring together this practice of stubborn misinterpretation with one of its consequences: the reduction of human beings to one-dimensional functionaries in an inflexible social order. Just as Dimmesdale must remain an example of piety—no matter how one has to stretch the facts—so, too, must Hester remain either a scapegoat or a negative example. She is not allowed to receive forgiveness.

CHAPTERS XIII–XIV

SUMMARY — CHAPTER XIII: ANOTHER VIEW OF HESTER
Seven years have passed since Pearl's birth. Hester has become more active in society. She brings food to the doors of the poor, she nurses the sick, and she is a source of aid in times of trouble. She is still frequently made an object of scorn, but more people are beginning to interpret the "A" on her chest as meaning "Able" rather than "Adulterer." Hester herself has also changed. She is no longer a tender and passionate woman; rather, burned by the "red-hot brand" of the letter, she has become "a bare and harsh outline" of her former self. She has become more speculative, thinking about how something is "amiss" in Pearl, about what it means to be a woman in her society, and about the harm she may be causing Dimmesdale by keeping Chillingworth's identity secret.

SUMMARY — CHAPTER XIV: HESTER AND THE PHYSICIAN
Hester resolves to ask Chillingworth to stop tormenting the minister. One day she and Pearl encounter him near the beach, gathering plants for his medicines. When Hester approaches him, he tells her with a smirk that he has heard "good tidings" of her, and that in fact the town fathers have recently considered allowing her to remove the scarlet letter. Hester rebuffs Chillingworth's insincere friendliness, telling him that the letter cannot be removed by human authority. Divine providence, she says, will make it fall from her chest when it is time for it to do so. She then informs Chillingworth that she feels it is time to tell the minister the truth about Chillingworth's

identity. From their conversation, it is clear that Chillingworth now knows with certainty that Dimmesdale was Hester's lover and that Hester is aware of his knowledge.

A change comes over Chillingworth's face, and the narrator notes that the old doctor has transformed himself into the very embodiment of evil. In a spasm of self-awareness, Chillingworth realizes how gnarled and mentally deformed he has become. He recalls the old days, when he was a benevolent scholar. He has now changed from a human being into a vengeful fiend, a mortal man who has lost his "human heart." Saying that she bears the blame for Chillingworth's tragic transformation, Hester begs him to relent in his revenge and become a human being again. The two engage in an argument over who is responsible for the current state of affairs. Chillingworth insists that his revenge and Hester's silence are "[their] fate." "Let the black flower blossom as it may!" he exclaims to her. "Now go thy ways, and deal as thou wilt with yonder man."

ANALYSIS — CHAPTERS XIII–XIV

Identity emerges as an important theme in this section of the novel. The ways in which a society tries to define a person are often at odds with the way that individual defines him- or herself. As the community reinterprets the scarlet letter, Hester once again has an identity thrust upon her by her fellow townspeople. The meaning of the letter can vary with the desires and needs of the community, because the letter does not signify any essential truth in itself. Like the meteor in Chapter XII, it simply serves to reinforce popular opinion.

Hester's improved reputation among the townspeople would seem to speak to the community's generosity of heart, its wisdom and compassion. Yet, because Puritan doctrine elevated faith and predestination over good works, no amount of good deeds can counteract sin; one must be ranked among the chosen. Thus, in a religious context, Hester's work in the community is futile. Although the community may acknowledge her intentions as good, it will never consider her divinely forgiven, and thus its members cannot forgive her in their own hearts. In the end, this is a society that privileges a pure and untainted soul above an actively good human being. Taken to an extreme, a doctrine that prizes faith over good works may mean that, in terms of everyday life, the pursuit of a transcendent heaven results in a hell on earth.

The town's reevaluation of Hester is also significant for what it says about Hester herself, about the change she has undergone in

earning it. The people of Boston believe that Hester's charitable behaviors are the result of their system working properly. They think
that their chosen punishment for her, the scarlet letter, has effectively humbled her as planned. In reality, "the scarlet letter [has] not
done its office." Hester has become almost an automaton: unwom-
anly, cold, and uncommunicative. The scarlet letter has not led her
to contemplate her sin and possible salvation. Rather, it has led her
to unholy speculations—thoughts of suicide and ruminations about
the unfair lot of women. In fact, Hester's protofeminist thinking
has led her to realize that she need not accept or pay attention to
the town's assessment of her at all. She refused to flee Boston when
Pearl was an infant because at the time she did not believe that her
fellow men and women should have the power to judge her. Now,
Hester refuses to remove the scarlet letter—she understands that
its removal would be as meaningless as its original placement. Her
identity and, she believes, her soul's salvation are matters that are
between her and God.

Hester's new insight into society's right to determine the lives
and identities of individuals is emphasized in her conversations
with Chillingworth. Hester feels that her soul is committed to
Dimmesdale rather than to Chillingworth, even though Chillingworth is legally her husband. She believes that a deeply felt interac-
tion between two people is more "real" than the church ceremony
that bound her to Chillingworth. She and Dimmesdale are bound by
mutual sin, and although this may seem a "marriage of evil," it also
unites them in their common humanity. Chillingworth, on the other
hand, views his actions as necessitated and sanctioned by his church
and by his God. In direct contrast to Hester, he sees the social and
religious orders as supreme.

CHAPTERS XV–XVI

SUMMARY — CHAPTER XV: HESTER AND PEARL
As Chillingworth walks away, Hester goes to find Pearl. She realizes
that, although it is a sin to do so, she hates her husband. If she once
thought she was happy with him, it was only self-delusion. Pearl has
been playing in the tide pools down on the beach. Pretending to be
a mermaid, she puts eelgrass on her chest in the shape of an "A,"
one that is "freshly green, instead of scarlet." Pearl hopes that her
mother will ask her about the letter, and Hester does inquire whether
Pearl understands the meaning of the symbol on her mother's chest.

They proceed to discuss the meaning of the scarlet letter. Pearl connects the letter to Dimmesdale's frequent habit of clutching his hand over his heart, and Hester is unnerved by her daughter's perceptiveness. She realizes the child is too young to know the truth and decides not to explain the significance of the letter to her. Pearl is persistent, though, and for the next several days she harangues her mother about the letter and about the minister's habit of reaching for his heart.

SUMMARY—CHAPTER XVI: A FOREST WALK

> *"Mother," said little Pearl, "the sunshine does not love you. It runs away and hides itself, because it is afraid of something on your bosom. . . . It will not flee from me; for I wear nothing on my bosom yet!"*
>
> (See QUOTATIONS, p. 57)

Intent upon telling Dimmesdale the truth about Chillingworth's identity, Hester waits for the minister in the forest, because she has heard that he will be passing through on the way back from visiting a Native American settlement. Pearl accompanies her mother and romps in the sunshine along the way. Curiously, the sunshine seems to shun Hester. As they wait for Dimmesdale by a brook, Pearl asks Hester to tell her about the "Black Man" and his connection to the scarlet letter. She has overheard an old woman discussing the midnight excursions of Mistress Hibbins and others, and the woman mentioned that Hester's scarlet letter is the mark of the "Black Man." When Pearl sees Dimmesdale's figure emerging from the wood, she asks whether the approaching person is the "Black Man." Hester, wanting privacy, tries to hurry Pearl off into the woods to play, but Pearl, both scared of and curious about the "Black Man," wants to stay. Exasperated, Hester exclaims, "It is no Black Man! . . . It is the minister!" Pearl scurries off, but not before wondering aloud whether the minister clutches his heart because the "Black Man" has left a mark there too.

ANALYSIS—CHAPTERS XV–XVI

These chapters return the reader to the romance world of preternaturally aware children and enchanted forests. Pearl has cleverly discerned the relationship between her mother's mark of shame and the minister's ailment, which share one obvious characteristic—their physical location upon the body. None of the townspeople has made the connection that Pearl now makes because they would never suspect their pastor to be capable of such a sin. Again, we see the problem with the Puritan "reading" of the world: intent on preserving the functional aspects of their society (i.e., the minister as an icon of purity), the people of Boston refuse to make what would seem to be an obvious set of connections between Hester's situation and the minister's mysterious torments. Pearl is too young to understand sex, adultery, or shame, but she is not blind, and she has intuitively understood the link between Hester and Dimmesdale for some time. She devises her green "A" as a deliberate test of her mother because she does not know why her mother is shunned and wants an explanation.

The best explanation Hester has for her daughter is to tell her that she has indeed met the "Black Man" and that the scarlet letter is his mark, as the old woman has said. The discussions in the last four chapters of the identity of the "Black Man" suggest a profound confusion among the characters about the nature of evil, the definition of which is an important theme in this book. Hester comes to a realization that her sins have resulted partially from the sins of others. For example, Chillingworth's willingness to manipulate a young and naïve Hester into marriage has led to the present hardness of her heart. Sin breeds sin, but not in the way the Puritan divines would have it. Sin is not a contamination but, at least in Hester's case, a response to hurt, loneliness, and the selfishness of others. Thus, the sources of evil are many and varied, as Pearl demonstrates in her identification of both Chillingworth and Dimmesdale as potential incarnations of the "Black Man."

The figure of Mistress Hibbins further complicates the picture of sin and evil in these chapters. As a witch participating in midnight rituals that directly invoke the "Black Man," one would expect her to be the very embodiment of sin. But it is possible that Mistress Hibbins is representative not so much of pure evil but of the society she initially appears to be subverting: although she knows she will eventually be executed as a witch, at this point Mistress Hibbins is reaping the benefits of Puritan society's hypocrisy. It is notable that she appears in the background of each of the scenes in which Hester faces some sort of crisis. She symbolizes this society's tolerance of, and even need for, malevolence. We are meant to see that her transgressions are simply more extreme versions of the evils done by men like her brother and Reverend Wilson. The fact that her behavior goes unpunished forces the reader to question whether it is Hester's lovemaking or the deeds of figures like Mistress Hibbins that really constitutes the greater threat to social stability.

Both Mistress Hibbins's late-night activities and Hester's and Pearl's soul-searching are set in the forest, a place that surrounds and yet stands in opposition to the town. The woods are wild and natural, unbound by any man-made rules or codes. Additionally, the forest is a place of privacy and intimacy, which contrasts markedly to the public spaces of the town. For these reasons, it is appropriate that Hester chooses to meet Dimmesdale in the woods, through which he will pass in transition between two human extremes—the repressed, codified Puritan town and the comparatively "wild" and "natural" Indian settlement. As an intermediary between the two, the forest serves as a space between repression and chaos, between condemnation and total liberty. It should provide a balance that is ideal for a reasoned exchange between the former lovers. Nature itself, however, seems to be signaling that what is to take place will not be a simple illumination of truth. The sunlight seems to be avoiding Hester deliberately as she and Pearl walk through the forest. If, as it frequently does, light symbolizes truth, then this strange natural phenomenon appears to be suggesting that Hester is avoiding, or will not find, the "truth" that she seeks to convey to Dimmesdale. Indeed, the next chapters will show this to be the case.

Chapters XVII–XVIII

Summary — Chapter XVII: The Pastor and His Parishioner

In the forest, Hester and Dimmesdale are finally able to escape both the public eye and Chillingworth. They join hands and sit in a secluded spot near a brook. Hester tells Dimmesdale that Chillingworth is her husband. This news causes a "dark transfiguration" in Dimmesdale, and he begins to condemn Hester, blaming her for his suffering. Hester, unable to bear his harsh words, pulls him to her chest and buries his face in the scarlet letter as she begs his pardon. Dimmesdale eventually forgives her, realizing that Chillingworth is a worse sinner than either of them. The minister now worries that Chillingworth, who knows of Hester's intention to reveal his secret, will expose them publicly. Hester tells the minister not to worry. She insists, though, that Dimmesdale free himself from the old man's power. The former lovers plot to steal away on a ship to Europe, where they can live with Pearl as a family.

SUMMARY—CHAPTER XVIII: A FLOOD OF SUNSHINE

The scarlet letter was [Hester's] passport into regions where other women dared not tread. Shame, Despair, Solitude! These had been her teachers, —stern and wild ones, —and they had made her strong, but taught her much amiss.

(See QUOTATIONS, *p. 58)*

The decision to move to Europe energizes both Dimmesdale and Hester. Dimmesdale declares that he can feel joy once again, and Hester throws the scarlet letter from her chest. Having cast off her "stigma," Hester regains some of her former, passionate beauty, and she lets down her hair and smiles. Sunlight, which as Pearl has pointed out stays away from her mother as though it fears her scarlet letter, suddenly brightens the forest. Hester speaks to Dimmesdale about Pearl and is ecstatic that father and daughter will be able to know one another. She calls their daughter, who has been playing among the forest creatures, to join them. Pearl approaches warily.

ANALYSIS—CHAPTERS XVII–XVIII

The encounter in the forest is the first time the reader sees Hester and Dimmesdale in an intimate setting. Hester is moved to call the minister by his first name, and the two join hands. They refer to the initial days of their romance as a "consecration," which suggests that they see their "sin" as having been no more than the fulfillment of a natural law. Up to this point, the narrator withheld any sentimental and tender aspects of the couple's relationship from the reader, which enabled him to focus on issues of punishment and social order. Now that the reader has had time to develop a strong feeling about this society's way of dealing with its problems, the narrator begins to complicate his treatment of sin as a theme. In previous chapters, the narrative has begun a subtle reevaluation of what constitutes sin. Hester and Chillingworth have discussed blame and responsibility, Mistress Hibbins has been introduced, and the narrator has provided commentary throughout on the hypocrisy of various figures. Here, though, Dimmesdale posits a hierarchy of sin, as he directly proclaims that Chillingworth's vengefulness is far worse than any adultery. This is the first official recognition in the text of any sort of alternative to the Puritan order, be it natural or intellectual.

Because of her alienation from society, Hester has taken an "estranged point of view [toward] human institutions." She has been able to think for herself, thanks to the scarlet letter and its dose of "Shame, Despair [and] Solitude." She seems to have developed an understanding of a sort of "natural law," and it is according to her instinctive principles that she decides that she, Dimmesdale, and Pearl should flee to Europe. A distinction is made between "sin" and "evil." Sin, as represented by Hester's past, constitutes an injury against the social and moral order but not against other human beings directly. Although it leads to alienation, it also leads to knowledge. It is a breaking of the rules for the sake of happiness. Evil, on the other hand, can be found in the hearts of those like Chillingworth, who seek no one's happiness—not even their own—and desire only the injury of others.

Dimmesdale reacts with "joy" to the planned escape, but it is unclear whether they have made the right decision or are entering into further sin. Because their two sets of principles differ drastically, Pearl's analysis of Hester and Dimmesdale is important in these chapters. Uncontaminated by society, Pearl is strongly associated with the natural world and therefore with truth. Hester believes that Pearl will provide the cement for her illegitimate relationship with Dimmesdale because, as their child, she naturally connects them. Yet, when Hester beckons Pearl to come to her, the child does not recognize her own mother. With her hair down and the letter gone, Hester doubtlessly looks different, and Pearl may read her mother's abandonment of the scarlet letter as an omen of her own abandonment. As Pearl is the one character in the narrative who has access to "truth," her unwillingness to respond to her mother suggests that there is something wrong with Hester and Dimmesdale's plan. One could view the couple's planned escape to Europe as a defeat—they have succumbed to the society that polices them and to the "sin" that has constantly threatened to overtake them.

CHAPTERS XIX–XX

SUMMARY—CHAPTER XIX: THE CHILD AT THE BROOK-SIDE
Hester calls to Pearl to join her and Dimmesdale. From the other side of the brook, Pearl eyes her parents with suspicion. She refuses to come to her mother, pointing at the empty place on Hester's chest where the scarlet letter used to be. Hester has to pin the letter back on and effect a transformation back into her old, sad self before Pearl will cross the creek. In her mother's arms, Pearl kisses Hester and, seemingly out of spite, also kisses the scarlet letter. Hester tries

to encourage Pearl to embrace Dimmesdale as well, although she does not tell her that the minister is her father. Pearl, aware that the adults seem to have made some sort of arrangement, asks, "Will he go back with us, hand in hand, we three together, into the town?" Because Dimmesdale will not, Pearl rebuffs his subsequent kiss on the forehead. She runs to the brook and attempts to wash it off.

SUMMARY — CHAPTER XX: THE MINISTER IN A MAZE

As the minister returns to town, he can hardly believe the change in his fortunes. He and Hester have decided to go to Europe, since it offers more anonymity and a better environment for Dimmesdale's fragile health. Through her charity work, Hester has become acquainted with the crew of a ship that is to depart for England in four days, and the couple plans to secure passage on this vessel. Tempted to announce to all he sees, "I am not the man for whom you take me! I left him yonder in the forest," Dimmesdale now finds things that were once familiar, including himself, to seem strange.

As he passes one of the church elders on his way through town, the minister can barely control his urge to utter blasphemous statements. He then encounters an elderly woman who is looking for a small tidbit of spiritual comfort. To her he nearly blurts out a devastating "unanswerable argument against the immortality of the human soul," but something stops him, and the widow totters away satisfied. He next ignores a young woman whom he has recently converted to the church because he fears that his strange state of mind will lead him to plant some corrupting germ in her innocent heart. Passing one of the sailors from the ship on which he plans to escape, Dimmesdale has the impulse to engage with him in a round of oaths; this comes only shortly after an encounter with a group of children, whom the minister nearly teaches some "wicked words." Finally, Dimmesdale runs into Mistress Hibbins, who chuckles at him and offers herself as an escort the next time he visits the forest. This interchange disturbs Dimmesdale and suggests to him that he may have made a bargain with Mistress Hibbins's master, the Devil.

When he reaches his house, Dimmesdale tells Chillingworth that he has no more need of the physician's drugs. Chillingworth becomes wary but is afraid to ask Dimmesdale outright if the minister knows his real identity. Dimmesdale has already started to write the sermon he is expected to deliver in three days for Election Day (a religious as well as civil holiday that marks the opening of the year's legislative session). In light of his new view of humanity, he now throws his former manuscript in the fire and writes a newer and better sermon.

ANALYSIS — CHAPTERS XIX–XX

Hester and Dimmesdale's encounter serves to further complicate what is already a morally ambiguous situation. The sun shines on the couple when Hester removes the scarlet letter, suggesting that nature, God, or both favor their plan. Pearl, on the contrary, cannot accept this new, happier version of her mother. When she forces Hester to reattach the letter to her breast, Hester's beauty immediately dissolves, "like fading sunshine," making it seem as if Pearl is wrong to make her mother reassume her old identity. But the reader has already learned to associate Pearl with a special sort of insight, and thus it does not seem likely that Pearl errs here. Indeed, once Pearl rejoins her parents, it becomes apparent that she is right to be skeptical. She asks Dimmesdale to publicly acknowledge his relationship to her, and he refuses.

When added to the fact that the couple plans to flee to Europe, Pearl's instinctual displeasure with the changes that have taken place in the forest suggests that Hester and Dimmesdale are not operating according to a newer, better moral code but are instead trying to find new ways to defy the same old social rules. The Puritans fled Europe out of the desire to live in a place where they would not need to hide their religious affiliations or fear the sanctions of others. Within the novel, they simply seem to have re-created the old order in the new world. Likewise, Hester and Dimmesdale are failing in their attempt to follow a higher truth. The most damning evidence of this is the fact that Dimmesdale is pleased that he will be able to stay in Boston long enough to preach the sermon for Election Day, a holiday that celebrates the forces that have tried to destroy the former lovers. Seemingly without irony, he finds it the appropriate conclusion to his career. The struggle between individual identity and social identity remains an important theme.

The thematic connection of sin with alienation and knowledge continues in these chapters. Dimmesdale returns to the village with a changed perspective. His experience in the wilderness has led him to question every aspect of his existence, and all of his usual behaviors are reversed. Dimmesdale walks a fine line between revelation and knowledge on the one hand, and destruction and evil on the other. His devilish impulses—to say that the human soul is mortal

THE SCARLET LETTER ❦ 49

and that oaths and curses are the best response to a cruel world—might be revelations. They could also be insidious lies that will lead to his damnation.

When Dimmesdale ignores the young woman whom he encounters on the street, he clings to the values he ought, according to his newfound beliefs, to reject. Had he spoken to the young woman, he could have offered her a more realistic version of human experience. Instead, he allows her to remain part of a system he has come to accept as corrupt, because he still lazily believes that the church offers her a way to salvation. Moreover, Dimmesdale worries that encountering her now, after his time in the woods, would somehow contaminate her, but what he fails to acknowledge fully is that the contamination has already occurred. The text makes clear that he has used the young woman's sexual attraction to him to win her over to the church.

CHAPTERS XXI–XXII

SUMMARY—CHAPTER XXI: THE NEW ENGLAND HOLIDAY
Echoing the novel's beginning, the narrator describes another public gathering in the marketplace. But this time the purpose is to celebrate the installation of a new governor, not to punish Hester Prynne. The celebration is relatively sober, but the townspeople's "Elizabethan" love of splendor lends an air of pageantry to the goings-on. As they wait in the marketplace among an assorted group of townsfolk, Native Americans, and sailors from the ship that is to take Hester and Dimmesdale to Europe, Pearl asks Hester whether the strange minister who does not want to acknowledge them in public will hold out his hands to her as he did at the brook. Lost in her thoughts and largely ignored by the crowd, Hester is imagining herself defiantly escaping from her long years of dreariness and isolation. Her sense of anticipation is shattered, however, when one of the sailors casually reveals that Chillingworth will be joining them on their passage because the ship needs a doctor and Chillingworth has told the captain that he is a member of Hester's party. Hester looks up to see Chillingworth standing across the marketplace, smirking at her.

SUMMARY—CHAPTER XXII: THE PROCESSION

"Mother," said [Pearl], "was that the same minister
that kissed me by the brook?"
   "Hold thy peace, dear little Pearl!" whispered
[Hester]. "We must not always talk in the market-place
of what happens to us in the forest."
                              (See QUOTATIONS, *p. 59)*

The majestic procession passes through the marketplace. A company of armored soldiers is followed by a group of the town fathers, whose stolid and dour characters are prominently displayed. Hester is disheartened to see the richness and power of Puritan tradition displayed with such pomp. She and other onlookers notice that Dimmesdale, who follows the town leaders, looks healthier and more energetic than he has in some time. Although only a few days have passed since he kissed her forehead next to the forest brook, Pearl barely recognizes the minister. She tells Hester that she is tempted to approach the man and bestow a kiss of her own, and Hester scolds her. Dimmesdale's apparent vigor saddens Hester because it makes him seem remote. She begins to question the wisdom of their plans. Mistress Hibbins, very elaborately dressed, comes to talk to Hester about Dimmesdale. Saying that she knows those who serve the Black Man, Mistress Hibbins refers to what she calls the minister's "mark" and declares that it will soon, like Hester's, be plain to all. Suggesting that the Devil is Pearl's real father, Mistress Hibbins invites the child to go on a witch's ride with her at some point in the future. The narrator interrupts his narration of the celebration to note that Mistress Hibbins will soon be executed as a witch.

After the old woman leaves, Hester takes her place at the foot of the scaffold to listen to Dimmesdale's sermon, which has commenced inside the meetinghouse. Pearl, who has been wandering around the marketplace, returns to give her mother a message from the ship's master—Chillingworth says he will make the arrangements for bringing Dimmesdale on board, so Hester should attend only to herself and her child. While Hester worries about this new development, she suddenly realizes that everyone around her—both those who are familiar with her scarlet letter and those who are not—is staring at her.

Analysis — Chapters XXI–XXII

These chapters set the stage for the dramatic resolution of the plot. Tension is created by the text's establishment of a number of conflicts between outward appearances and inward states. We await the inevitable collision and collapse of external and internal, public and private. In her final hours of wearing the scarlet letter, Hester has begun to anticipate her imminent freedom from shame, yet the crowd is quick to remind her that the letter has not yet lost its power of public proclamation. Their transfixed stares emphasize the badge's persistent visibility, even though, by this point in time, one would no longer expect it to draw much attention. Such gazes continue to exert great force over Hester, and her feelings of escape from them prove premature. Meanwhile, Dimmesdale's outer appearance of health, though it may accurately reflect his joy at the thought of his plan with Hester, fails to convey the shadow of past suffering that surely continues to haunt him. While he prepares to pronounce one of the most powerful sermons of his life, his holy words issue from an inner state of what the Puritan elders would consider sin. All of the primary characters in the book, save perhaps Pearl, maintain a secret, something they are hiding as they stand in the public realm of the marketplace. The revelation of these secrets will bring the plot to its climactic explosion.

The pageantry that marks the Election Day festivities provides an appropriate backdrop for the plot's suspense-building events. The loud music, the costumes, and the display of power are all reminders of the hypocrisy at the heart of Puritan society. The Puritans came from and shunned Elizabethan England, a culture that loved and yearned for ostentatious opulence. It seems that the Puritans' repression of their own desires for extravagant displays may have only intensified the power images have over them. The exceptionally straightforward revelry serves to highlight the fact that the desire for splendor has always existed. In effect, the Puritans have re-created the aesthetic of the society from which they tried to escape.

Hester, the sailors, and the Native Americans are meaningful symbols of subversion. Because the sailors are perceived as facing grave terrors on the open sea, society tends to overlook their eccentric behavior, and they can carry on in active defiance of convention. The presence of the Native Americans, who are positioned at an even greater distance from mainstream colonist society, adds more weight to the novel's social critique. Unaware of the story behind the scarlet letter, they think its wearer is a person of great importance. Their reaction highlights the arbitrary nature of this important sign.

Yet, these figures of subversion in the marketplace ultimately serve to suggest the absence of any true alternatives. To the Puritans, the holiday display, the sailors, and the Native Americans constitute the exceptions that prove the rule of Puritan social order. The return of the action to the novel's initial setting—the public space before the scaffold where Hester originally received her punishment—foreshadows the fact that Hester's physical and moral emancipation will be thwarted. As Hester stands apart from her fellow Bostonians—no one wants to stand too close to her—she once more becomes an example to keep others in line. Unable to exercise her free will as a human being, Hester stands no chance for escape. Chillingworth and the town elders are part of a larger, self-serving evil that can overcome any challenges by assigning them new meanings to fit its own purposes. Dimmesdale, too, becomes once more a part of this dominant order; hence Hester's sense that he seems "remote." Dimmesdale, like the other townspeople, reminds Hester that resistance is futile.

Chapters XXIII–XXIV

Summary—Chapter XXIII: The Revelation of the Scarlet Letter

Dimmesdale finishes his Election Day sermon, which focuses on the relationship between God and the communities of mankind, "with a special reference to the New England which they [are] here planting in the wilderness." Dimmesdale has proclaimed that the people of New England will be chosen by God, and the crowd is understandably moved by the sermon. As they file out of the meeting hall, the people murmur to each other that the sermon was the minister's best, most inspired, and most truthful ever. As they move toward the town hall for the evening feast, Dimmesdale sees Hester and hesitates. Turning toward the scaffold, he calls to Hester and Pearl to join him. Deaf to Chillingworth's attempt to stop him, Dimmesdale mounts the scaffold with Hester and Pearl. He declares that God has led him there. The crowd stares. Dimmesdale leans on Hester for support and begins his confession, calling himself "the one sinner of the world." After he concludes, he stands upright without Hester's help and tells everyone to see that he, like Hester, has a red stigma. Tearing away his ministerial garments from his breast, Dimmesdale reveals what we take to be some sort of mark—the narrator demurs, saying that it would be "irreverent to describe [the] revelation"—and then sinks onto the scaffold. The crowd recoils in shock, and Chillingworth cries out, "Thou hast escaped me!" Pearl finally bestows on Dimmesdale the kiss she has withheld from him. The minister and Hester then exchange words. She asks him whether they will spend their afterlives together, and he responds that God will decide whether they will receive any further punishment for breaking His sacred law. The minister bids her farewell and dies.

SUMMARY — CHAPTER XXIV: CONCLUSION

> *[T]he scarlet letter ceased to be a stigma which*
> *attracted the world's scorn and bitterness, and became*
> *a type of something to be sorrowed over, and looked*
> *upon with awe, and yet with reverence, too.*
>
> *(See* QUOTATIONS, *p. 60)*

The book's narrator discusses the events that followed Dimmesdale's death and reports on the fates of the other major characters. Apparently, those who witnessed the minister's death cannot agree upon what exactly it was that they saw. Most say they saw on his chest a scarlet letter exactly like Hester's. To their minds, it resulted from Chillingworth's poisonous magic, from the minister's self-torture, or from his inner remorse. Others say they saw nothing on his chest and that Dimmesdale's "revelation" was simply that any man, however holy or powerful, can be as guilty of sin as Hester. It is the narrator's opinion that this latter group is composed of Dimmesdale's friends, who are anxious to protect his reputation.

Left with no object for his malice, Chillingworth wastes away and dies within a year of the minister's passing, leaving a sizable inheritance to Pearl. Then, shortly after Chillingworth's death, Hester and Pearl disappear. In their absence, the story of the scarlet letter grows into a legend. The story proves so compelling that the town preserves the scaffold and Hester's cottage as material testaments to it. Many years later, Hester suddenly returns alone to live in the cottage and resumes her charity work. By the time of her death, the "A," which she still wears, has lost any stigma it may have had. Hester is buried in the King's Chapel graveyard, which is the burial ground for Puritan patriarchs. Her grave is next to Dimmesdale's, but far enough away to suggest that "the dust of the two sleepers had no right to mingle, even in death." They do, however, share a headstone. It bears a symbol that the narrator feels appropriately sums up the whole of the narrative: a scarlet letter "A" on a black background.

ANALYSIS — CHAPTERS XXIII–XXIV

This third and final scaffold scene serves as a catharsis, as all unsettled matters are given resolution. Pearl acquires a father, Dimmesdale finally confesses, and Chillingworth definitively loses his chance for revenge. Moreover, despite the fact that the resolution takes place before the assembled townspeople, the Puritan elders have no power to judge or punish in this situation. Instead, Dimmesdale serves as his own prosecutor and judge. He apparently wills his own death, thereby breaking away from Puritan morals. He also provides a commentary on them, addressing the novel's main themes of sin, evil, and identity within society. One might think that the people's shock at their minister's secret life would provoke them into contemplation of their punitive system. That is, if Dimmesdale is capable of such a sin, then surely every individual must be; perhaps sinfulness should be acknowledged as an inescapable element of the human condition.

However, no such reconsideration takes place. The old order regains control soon after Dimmesdale's death. Although many claim to have seen a scarlet "A" on Dimmesdale's chest, others read the minister's confession as an intentional allegorical performance. It is this latter group, which argues that Dimmesdale meant to deliver a lesson on sin and was not confessing to any actual wrongdoing, that reestablishes the old ways. In their view, Dimmesdale meant to teach his parishioners that all men have the potential for evil, not that evil is a necessary part of man. Correspondingly, the conservatives believe, society need only renew its vigilance against evil rather than reconsider its very conception of evil. Even in his defiance, then, Dimmesdale is appropriated by the Puritan system as a means of reinforcing its preestablished messages.

However, this victory for the entrenched ways seems to be only temporary. It is no surprise that Chillingworth dies, because the "leech's" source of vitality has been removed. Hester's and Pearl's fates are more complicated. Given an "earthly father" for the first time, Pearl finally, according to the narrator, becomes "human." It is as though Pearl has existed up to this point solely to torment her parents and expose the truth—she is, after all, the direct result of their sin. The final acknowledgment of that sin has freed her. It has "developed her sympathies" and made her an autonomous and fully "human" being. Pearl returns to Europe and marries into an aristocratic family. Notably, she does not go to England, which is the society against which the Puritans define themselves. Pearl opts out of this binary altogether, finding a home in a place where the social structure is well established and need not rely on a dogmatic adherence to rules in order to protect its existence.

Unlike Pearl, Hester can never escape her role as an emblem of something larger. She leaves Boston, presumably to give her daughter a better chance at a happy life, but in so doing ensures that her scarlet letter will become a "legend" and take on a kind of existence of its own. Having sacrificed her humanity and her individuality to her child, and to the letter on her chest, Hester now becomes a spokeswoman for larger issues. She becomes an advocate for women and takes on a role in the community similar to that of a minister: she cares for and attends to the spiritual needs of her fellow human beings. Hester's burial speaks to the eventual sacrifice of her private self to her public, symbolic role. Although she and Dimmesdale are together at last, the distance between their graves and the design of their shared headstone seem to call out for interpretive readings. The simple romantic relationship between them is overshadowed by its larger representations.

By the time Hester dies, the meaning of the scarlet letter on her chest has become confused and ambiguous. While it gives her authority and even respectability among some people, it will always mark her as guilty of what society still considers a sin. The fates of the other characters also suggest that it is not always easy to differentiate between hate and love, between essential identity and assigned symbolism, or between sin and righteousness.

Important Quotations Explained

1. "A writer of story-books! What kind of a business in life,—what mode of glorifying God, or being serviceable to mankind in his day and generation,—may that be? Why, the degenerate fellow might as well have been a fiddler!" Such are the compliments bandied between my great-grandsires and myself, across the gulf of time! And yet, let them scorn me as they will, strong traits of their nature have intertwined themselves with mine.

This passage comes from the introductory section of *The Scarlet Letter,* in which the narrator details how he decided to write his version of Hester Prynne's story. Part of his interest in the story is personal—he is descended from the original Puritan settlers of Massachusetts. Like Hester, the narrator both affirms and resists Puritan values. He is driven to write, yet the Puritan in him sees the frivolity in such an endeavor: what good, after all, can come of writing this story? Yet in that very question lies the significance of this tale, which interrogates the conflict between individual impulses and systematized social codes. The narrator finds Hester Prynne compelling because she represents America's past, but also because her experiences reflect his own dilemmas. Thus, for the narrator, the act of writing about Hester becomes not a trivial activity but a means of understanding himself and his social context.

2.   "Mother," said little Pearl, "the sunshine does not love
     you. It runs away and hides itself, because it is afraid of
     something on your bosom. . . . It will not flee from me, for
     I wear nothing on my bosom yet!"
         "Nor ever will, my child, I hope," said Hester.
         "And why not, mother?" asked Pearl, stopping
     short. . . . "Will it not come of its own accord, when I am
     a woman grown?"

This quote, taken from Chapter XVI, "A Forest Walk," is illustrative of the role Pearl plays in the text. It is also a meditation on the
significance of the scarlet letter as a symbol and an exposition of the
connection between sin and humanness—one of the novel's most
important themes.

Pearl is frequently aware of things that others do not see, and here
she presciently identifies the scarlet letter on her mother's bosom
with the metaphorical (and in this case also literal) lack of sunshine
in her mother's life. Because she is just a child, Pearl often does not
understand the ramifications of the things she sees. She frequently
reveals truths only indirectly by asking pointed questions. These
queries make her mother uncomfortable and contribute to the text's
suspense. Here Pearl is assuming, as children often do, that her
mother is representative of all adults. Her question suggests that she
thinks that all grown women wear a scarlet letter or its equivalent.
Surely, Pearl has noticed that the other women in town don't wear
scarlet letters. But, on a more figurative level, her question suggests
that sin—that which the scarlet letter is intended to represent—is an
inevitable part of being a mature human being.

QUOTATIONS

3.   But Hester Prynne, with a mind of native courage and
       activity, and for so long a period not merely estranged,
       but outlawed, from society, had habituated herself to such
       latitude of speculation as was altogether foreign to the
       clergyman. She had wandered, without rule or guidance, in
       a moral wilderness. . . . The scarlet letter was her passport
       into regions where other women dared not tread. Shame,
       Despair, Solitude! These had been her teachers,—stern and
       wild ones,—and they had made her strong, but taught her
       much amiss.

These are the narrator's reflections at the beginning of Chapter
XVIII, "A Flood of Sunshine." The quotation concerns the theme of
sin and knowledge that is so central to *The Scarlet Letter*. Over the
course of their first significant conversation in many years, Hester
and Dimmesdale decide to run away to Europe together. The minister is still in a state of shock, but Hester accepts their decision with
relative equanimity. One result of her "sin" has been her profound
alienation from society—she has been forced into the role of phi-
losopher. Although the narrator tries to claim that her speculations
have led her "amiss," it is clear from his tone that he admires her
intellectual bravery. It is deeply ironic, too, that it is her punishment,
which was intended to help her atone and to make her an example
for the community, that has led her into a "moral wilderness" devoid
of "rule or guidance." Finally, this passage is a good example of the
eloquent, high-flown yet measured style that the narrator frequently
adopts when considering the moral or philosophical ramifications
of a situation.

QUOTATIONS

4. "Mother," said [Pearl], "was that the same minister that
    kissed me by the brook?"
    "Hold thy peace, dear little Pearl!" whispered her
    mother. "We must not always talk in the market-place of
    what happens to us in the forest."

This conversation, which is described in Chapter XXII, takes place a
few days after Hester and Pearl's encounter with Dimmesdale in the
forest. It emphasizes the importance of physical settings in the novel
and evokes the motif of civilization versus the wilderness. Dimmesdale has just walked by Hester and Pearl as part of the Election
Day pageantry, and Pearl notices his changed appearance. Hester's
realization that different rules apply in the marketplace than in the
forest has more significant consequences than she realizes, making
this yet another ironic moment in the text. Hester primarily wishes
Pearl to maintain a sense of decorum and not reveal her mother's
secret and the family's plans to flee. On another level, though, Hester's statement suggests that plans made in the forest will not with-
stand the public scrutiny of the marketplace. What is possible in
the woods—a place of fantasy, possibility, and freedom—is not an
option in the heart of the Puritan town, where order, prescription,
and harsh punishment reign.

5.   But there was a more real life for Hester Prynne here,
     in New England, than in that unknown region where
     Pearl had found a home. Here had been her sin; here,
     her sorrow; and here was yet to be her penitence. She
     had returned, therefore, and resumed,—of her own free
     will, for not the sternest magistrate of that iron period
     would have imposed it,—resumed the symbol of which
     we have related so dark a tale. Never afterwards did it
     quit her bosom. But . . . the scarlet letter ceased to be a
     stigma which attracted the world's scorn and bitterness,
     and became a type of something to be sorrowed over, and
     looked upon with awe, and yet with reverence, too.

This passage, which appears in the novel's final chapter, concludes
the book's examination of the theme of individual identity in the
face of social judgments. After many years' absence, Hester has just
returned to her former home. She resumes wearing the scarlet letter because her past is an important part of her identity; it is not
something that should be erased or denied because someone else
has decided it is shameful. What Hester undergoes is more akin to
reconciliation than penitence. She creates a life in which the scarlet
letter is a symbol of adversity overcome and of knowledge gained
rather than a sign of failure or condemnation. She assumes control of her own identity, and in so doing she becomes an example
for others. She is not, however, the example of sin that she was
once intended to be. Rather, she is an example of redemption and
self-empowerment.

KEY FACTS

FULL TITLE
The Scarlet Letter

AUTHOR
Nathaniel Hawthorne

TYPE OF WORK
Novel

GENRE
Symbolic; semi-allegorical; historical fiction; romance (in the sense that it rejects realism in favor of symbols and ideas)

LANGUAGE
English

TIME AND PLACE WRITTEN
Salem and Concord, Massachusetts; late 1840s

DATE OF FIRST PUBLICATION
1850

PUBLISHER
Ticknor, Reed, and Fields

NARRATOR
The narrator is an unnamed customhouse surveyor who writes some two hundred years after the events he describes took place. He has much in common with Hawthorne but should not be taken as a direct mouthpiece for the author's opinions.

POINT OF VIEW
The narrator is omniscient, because he analyzes the characters and tells the story in a way that shows that he knows more about the characters than they know about themselves. Yet, he is also a subjective narrator, because he voices his own interpretations and opinions of things. He is clearly sympathetic to Hester and Dimmesdale.

TONE

Varies—contemplative and somewhat bitter in the introduction; thoughtful, fairly straightforward, yet occasionally tinged with irony in the body of the narrative

TENSE

The narrator employs the past tense to recount events that happened some two hundred years before his time, but he occasionally uses the present tense when he addresses his audience.

SETTING (TIME)

Middle of the seventeenth century

SETTING (PLACE)

Boston, Massachusetts

PROTAGONIST

Hester Prynne

MAJOR CONFLICT

Her husband having inexplicably failed to join her in Boston following their emigration from Europe, Hester Prynne engages in an extramarital affair with Arthur Dimmesdale. When she gives birth to a child, Hester invokes the condemnation of her community—a condemnation they manifest by forcing her to wear a letter "A" for "adulteror"—as well as the vengeful wrath of her husband, who has appeared just in time to witness her public shaming.

RISING ACTION

Dimmesdale stands by in silence as Hester suffers for the "sin" he helped to commit, though his conscience plagues him and affects his health. Hester's husband, Chillingworth, hides his true identity and, posing as a doctor to the ailing minister, tests his suspicions that Dimmesdale is the father of his wife's child, effectively exacerbating Dimmesdale's feelings of shame and thus reaping revenge.

CLIMAX

There are at least two points in *The Scarlet Letter* that could be identified as the book's "climax." The first is in Chapter XII, at the exact center of the book. As Dimmesdale watches a meteor trace a letter "A" in the sky, he confronts his role in

Hester's sin and realizes that he can no longer deny his deed
and its consequences. The key characters confront one another
when Hester and Pearl join Dimmesdale in an "electric chain"
as he holds his vigil on the marketplace scaffold, the location
of Hester's original public shaming. Chillingworth appears in
this scene as well. The other climactic scene occurs in Chapter
XXIII, at the end of the book. Here, the characters' secrets are
publicly exposed and their fates sealed. Dimmesdale, Hester,
and Chillingworth not only acknowledge their secrets to
themselves and to each other; they push these revelations to
such extremes that they all must leave the community in one
way or another.

FALLING ACTION

Depending on one's interpretation of which scene constitutes
the book's "climax," the falling action is either the course
of events that follow Chapter XII or the final reports on
Hester's and Pearl's lives after the deaths of Dimmesdale and
Chillingworth.

THEMES

Sin, experience, and the human condition; the nature of evil;
identity and society

MOTIFS

Civilization versus the wilderness; night versus day; evocative
names

SYMBOLS

The scarlet letter; the town scaffold; the meteor; Pearl; the
rosebush next to the prison door

FORESHADOWING

Foreshadowing is minimal, because the symbols tend to
coincide temporally with events, enriching their meaning rather
than anticipating their occurrence.

KEY FACTS

STUDY QUESTIONS

1. *Discuss the relationship between the scarlet letter and Hester's identity. Why does she repeatedly refuse to stop wearing the letter? What is the difference between the identity she creates for herself and the identity society assigns to her?*

For Hester, to remove the scarlet letter would be to acknowledge the power it has in determining who she is. The letter would prove to have successfully restricted her if she were to become a different person in its absence. Hester chooses to continue to wear the letter because she is determined to transform its meaning through her actions and her own self-perception—she wants to be the one who controls its meaning. Society tries to reclaim the letter's symbolism by deciding that the "A" stands for "Able," but Hester resists this interpretation. The letter symbolizes her own past deed and her own past decisions, and she is the one who will determine the meaning of those events. Upon her return from Europe at the novel's end, Hester has gained control over both her personal and her public identities. She has made herself into a symbol of feminine repression and charitable ideals, and she stands as a self-appointed reminder of the evils society can commit.

2.   *In what ways could* THE SCARLET LETTER *be read
     as a commentary on the era of American history it
     describes? How does Hawthorne's portrayal of Europe
     enter into this commentary? Could the book also be
     seen as embodying some of the aspects it attributes to
     the nation in which it was written?*

Typically, America is conceptualized as a place of freedom, where a
person's opportunities are limited only by his or her ambition and
ability—and not by his or her social status, race, gender, or other
circumstances of birth. In the Puritan society portrayed in the novel,
however, this is not the case. In fact, it is Europe, not America, that
the book presents as a place of potential. There, anonymity can
protect an individual and allow him or her to assume a new identity.
This unexpected inversion leads the characters and the reader to
question the principles of freedom and opportunity usually identified with America. Hester's experiences suggest that this country
is founded on the ideals of repression and confinement. Additionally, the narrator's own experiences, coming approximately two
hundred years after Hester's, confirm those of his protagonist. His
fellow customs officers owe their jobs to patronage and family connections, not to merit, and he has acquired his own position through
political allies. Thus, the customhouse is portrayed as an institu-
tion that embodies many of the principles that America supposedly
opposes.

   Much of the social hypocrisy presented in the book stems from
America's newness. Insecure in its social order, the new society is
trying to distance itself from its Anglican origins yet, at the same
time, reassure itself of its legitimacy and dignity. It is a difficult task
to "define" oneself as a land of self-defining individuals. But it is
this project of defining America that Hawthorne himself partially
undertakes in his novel. He aims to write a text that both embodies
and describes "Americanness."

3. *This novel makes extensive use of symbols. Discuss
    the difference between the Puritans' use of symbols
    (the meteor, for example) and the way that the
    narrator makes use of symbols. Do both have religious
    implications? Do symbols foreshadow events or
    simply comment on them after the fact? How do they
    help the characters understand their lives, and how do
    they help the reader understand Hawthorne's book?*

The Puritans in this book are constantly seeking out natural symbols, which they claim are messages from God. Yet these characters are not willing to accept any revelation at face value. They interpret the symbols only in ways that confirm their own preformulated ideas or opinions. The meteor that streaks the sky as Dimmesdale stands on the scaffold in Chapter XII is a good example of this phenomenon. To Dimmesdale and to the townspeople, the "A" that the meteor traces in the sky represents whatever notion already preoccupies them. To the minister, the meteor exposes his sin, while to the townspeople it confirms that the colony's former governor, who has just died, has gone to heaven and been made an angel.

For the narrator, on the other hand, symbols function to complicate reality rather than to confirm one's perception of it. The governor's garden, which Hester and Pearl see in Chapter VII, illustrates his tactic quite well. The narrator does not describe the garden in a way that reinforces the image of luxury and power that is present in his description of the rest of the governor's house. Rather, he writes that the garden, which was originally planted to look like an ornamental garden in the English style, is now full of weeds, thorns, and vegetables. The garden seems to contradict much of what the reader has been told about the governor's power and importance, and it suggests to us that the governor is an unfit caretaker, for people as well as for flowers. The absence of any flowers other than the thorny roses also hints that ideals are often accompanied by evil and pain. Confronted by the ambiguous symbol of the garden, we begin to look for other inconsistencies and for other examples of decay and disrepair in Puritan society.

How to Write
Literary Analysis

The Literary Essay: A Step-by-Step Guide

When you read for pleasure, your only goal is enjoyment. You might find yourself reading to get caught up in an exciting story, to learn about an interesting time or place, or just to pass time. Maybe you're looking for inspiration, guidance, or a reflection of your own life. There are as many different, valid ways of reading a book as there are books in the world.

When you read a work of literature in an English class, however, you're being asked to read in a special way: you're being asked to perform *literary analysis*. To analyze something means to break it down into smaller parts and then examine how those parts work, both individually and together. Literary analysis involves examining all the parts of a novel, play, short story, or poem—elements such as character, setting, tone, and imagery—and thinking about how the author uses those elements to create certain effects.

A literary essay isn't a book review: you're not being asked whether or not you liked a book or whether you'd recommend it to another reader. A literary essay also isn't like the kind of book report you wrote when you were younger, where your teacher wanted you to summarize the book's action. A high school- or college-level literary essay asks, "How does this piece of literature actually work?" "How does it do what it does?" and, "Why might the author have made the choices he or she did?"

The Seven Steps
No one is born knowing how to analyze literature; it's a skill you learn and a process you can master. As you gain more practice with this kind of thinking and writing, you'll be able to craft a method that works best for you. But until then, here are seven basic steps to writing a well-constructed literary essay:

1. *Ask questions*
2. *Collect evidence*
3. *Construct a thesis*

4. *Develop and organize arguments*
5. *Write the introduction*
6. *Write the body paragraphs*
7. *Write the conclusion*

1. Ask Questions

When you're assigned a literary essay in class, your teacher will often provide you with a list of writing prompts. Lucky you! Now all you have to do is choose one. Do yourself a favor and pick a topic that interests you. You'll have a much better (not to mention easier) time if you start off with something you enjoy thinking about. If you are asked to come up with a topic by yourself, though, you might start to feel a little panicked. Maybe you have too many ideas—or none at all. Don't worry. Take a deep breath and start by asking yourself these questions:

- **What struck you?** Did a particular image, line, or scene linger in your mind for a long time? If it fascinated you, chances are you can draw on it to write a fascinating essay.

- **What confused you?** Maybe you were surprised to see a character act in a certain way, or maybe you didn't understand why the book ended the way it did. Confusing moments in a work of literature are like a loose thread in a sweater: if you pull on it, you can unravel the entire thing. Ask yourself why the author chose to write about that character or scene the way he or she did and you might tap into some important insights about the work as a whole.

- **Did you notice any patterns?** Is there a phrase that the main character uses constantly or an image that repeats throughout the book? If you can figure out how that pattern weaves through the work and what the significance of that pattern is, you've almost got your entire essay mapped out.

- **Did you notice any contradictions or ironies?** Great works of literature are complex; great literary essays recognize and explain those complexities. Maybe the title (*Happy Days*) totally disagrees with the book's subject matter (hungry orphans dying in the woods). Maybe the main character acts one way around his family and a completely different way around his friends and associates. If you can find a way to explain a work's contradictory elements, you've got the seeds of a great essay.

At this point, you don't need to know exactly what you're going to say about your topic; you just need a place to begin your exploration. You can help direct your reading and brainstorming by formulating your topic as a *question,* which you'll then try to answer in your essay. The best questions invite critical debates and discussions, not just a rehashing of the summary. Remember, you're looking for something you can *prove or argue* based on evidence you find in the text. Finally, remember to keep the scope of your question in mind: is this a topic you can adequately address within the word or page limit you've been given? Conversely, is this a topic big enough to fill the required length?

GOOD QUESTIONS
"Are Romeo and Juliet's parents responsible for the deaths of their children?"

"Why do pigs keep showing up in LORD OF THE FLIES*?"*

"Are Dr. Frankenstein and his monster alike? How?"

BAD QUESTIONS
"What happens to Scout in TO KILL A MOCKINGBIRD*?"*

"What do the other characters in JULIUS CAESAR *think about Caesar?"*

"How does Hester Prynne in THE SCARLET LETTER *remind me of my sister?"*

---

2. COLLECT EVIDENCE
Once you know what question you want to answer, it's time to scour the book for things that will help you answer the question. Don't worry if you don't know what you want to say yet—right now you're just collecting ideas and material and letting it all percolate. Keep track of passages, symbols, images, or scenes that deal with your topic. Eventually, you'll start making connections between these examples and your thesis will emerge.

Here's a brief summary of the various parts that compose each and every work of literature. These are the elements that you will analyze in your essay, and which you will offer as evidence to support your arguments. For more on the parts of literary works, see the Glossary of Literary Terms at the end of this section.

LITERARY ANALYSIS

ELEMENTS OF STORY   These are the *what*s of the work—what happens, where it happens, and to whom it happens.

- **Plot:** All of the events and actions of the work.

- **Character:** The people who act and are acted upon in a literary work. The main character of a work is known as the *protagonist*.

- **Conflict:** The central tension in the work. In most cases, the protagonist wants something, while opposing forces (antagonists) hinder the protagonist's progress.

- **Setting:** When and where the work takes place. Elements of setting include location, time period, time of day, weather, social atmosphere, and economic conditions.

- **Narrator:** The person telling the story. The narrator may straightforwardly report what happens, convey the subjective opinions and perceptions of one or more characters, or provide commentary and opinion in his or her own voice.

- **Themes:** The main idea or message of the work—usually an abstract idea about people, society, or life in general. A work may have many themes, which may be in tension with one another.

ELEMENTS OF STYLE   These are the *how*s—how the characters speak, how the story is constructed, and how language is used throughout the work.

- **Structure and organization:** How the parts of the work are assembled. Some novels are narrated in a linear, chronological fashion, while others skip around in time. Some plays follow a traditional three- or five-act structure, while others are a series of loosely connected scenes. Some authors deliberately leave gaps in their works, leaving readers to puzzle out the missing information. A work's structure and organization can tell you a lot about the kind of message it wants to convey.

- **Point of view:** The perspective from which a story is told. In *first-person point of view*, the narrator involves him or herself in the story. ("I went to the store"; "We watched in horror as the bird slammed into the window.") A first-person narrator is usually the protagonist of the work, but not always. In *third-person point of view*, the narrator does not participate in the story. A third-person narrator may closely follow a specific character, recounting that individual character's thoughts or experiences, or it may be what we call an *omniscient* narrator. Omniscient narrators see and know all: they can witness any event in any time or place and are privy to the inner thoughts and feelings of all characters. Remember that the narrator and the author are not the same thing!

- **Diction:** Word choice. Whether a character uses dry, clinical language or flowery prose with lots of exclamation points can tell you a lot about his or her attitude and personality.

- **Syntax:** Word order and sentence construction. Syntax is a crucial part of establishing an author's narrative voice. Ernest Hemingway, for example, is known for writing in very short, straightforward sentences, while James Joyce characteristically wrote in long, incredibly complicated lines.

- **Tone:** The mood or feeling of the text. Diction and syntax often contribute to the tone of a work. A novel written in short, clipped sentences that use small, simple words might feel brusque, cold, or matter-of-fact.

- **Imagery:** Language that appeals to the senses, representing things that can be seen, smelled, heard, tasted, or touched.

- **Figurative language:** Language that is not meant to be interpreted literally. The most common types of figurative language are *metaphors* and *similes,* which compare two unlike things in order to suggest a similarity between them— for example, "All the world's a stage," or "The moon is like a ball of green cheese." (Metaphors say one thing *is* another thing; similes claim that one thing is *like* another thing.)

---

3. CONSTRUCT A THESIS

When you've examined all the evidence you've collected and know how you want to answer the question, it's time to write your thesis statement. A *thesis* is a claim about a work of literature that needs to be supported by evidence and arguments. The thesis statement is the heart of the literary essay, and the bulk of your paper will be spent trying to prove this claim. A good thesis will be:

- **Arguable.** "*The Great Gatsby* describes New York society in the 1920s" isn't a thesis—it's a fact.

- **Provable through textual evidence.** "*Hamlet* is a confusing but ultimately very well-written play" is a weak thesis because it offers the writer's personal opinion about the book. Yes, it's arguable, but it's not a claim that can be proved or supported with examples taken from the play itself.

- **Surprising.** "Both George and Lenny change a great deal in *Of Mice and Men*" is a weak thesis because it's obvious. A really strong thesis will argue for a reading of the text that is not immediately apparent.

- **Specific.** "Dr. Frankenstein's monster tells us a lot about the human condition" is *almost* a really great thesis statement, but it's still too vague. What does the writer mean by "a lot"? *How* does the monster tell us so much about the human condition?

GOOD THESIS STATEMENTS

Question: In *Romeo and Juliet*, which is more powerful in shaping the lovers' story: fate or foolishness?

Thesis: "Though Shakespeare defines Romeo and Juliet as 'star-crossed lovers' and images of stars and planets appear throughout the play, a closer examination of that celestial imagery reveals that the stars are merely witnesses to the characters' foolish activities and not the causes themselves."

Question: How does the bell jar function as a symbol in Sylvia Plath's *The Bell Jar*?

Thesis: "A bell jar is a bell-shaped glass that has three basic uses: to hold a specimen for observation, to contain gases, and to maintain a vacuum. The bell jar appears in each of these capacities in *The Bell Jar*, Plath's semi-autobiographical novel, and each appearances marks a different stage in Esther's mental breakdown."

Question: Would Piggy in *The Lord of the Flies* make a good island leader if he were given the chance?

Thesis: "Though the intelligent, rational, and innovative Piggy has the mental characteristics of a good leader, he ultimately lacks the social skills necessary to be an effective one. Golding emphasizes this point by giving Piggy a foil in the charismatic Jack, whose magnetic personality allows him to capture and wield power effectively, if not always wisely."

4. DEVELOP AND ORGANIZE ARGUMENTS

The reasons and examples that support your thesis will form the middle paragraphs of your essay. Since you can't really write your thesis statement until you know how you'll structure your argument, you'll probably end up working on steps 3 and 4 at the same time.

There's no single method of argumentation that will work in every context. One essay prompt might ask you to compare and contrast two characters, while another asks you to trace an image through a given work of literature. These questions require different kinds of answers and therefore different kinds of arguments. Below, we'll discuss three common kinds of essay prompts and some strategies for constructing a solid, well-argued case.

TYPES OF LITERARY ESSAYS

- **Compare and contrast**

  Compare and contrast the characters of Huck and Jim in THE ADVENTURES OF HUCKLEBERRY FINN.

  Chances are you've written this kind of essay before. In an academic literary context, you'll organize your arguments the same way you would in any other class. You can either go *subject by subject* or *point by point*. In the former, you'll discuss one character first and then the second. In the latter, you'll choose several traits (attitude toward life, social status, images and metaphors associated with the character) and devote a paragraph to each. You may want to use a mix of these two approaches—for example, you may want to spend a paragraph a piece broadly sketching Huck's and Jim's personalities before transitioning into a paragraph or two that describes a few key points of comparison. This can be a highly effective strategy if you want to make a counterintuitive argument—that, despite seeming to be totally different, the two objects being compared are actually similar in a very important way (or vice versa). Remember that your essay should reveal something fresh or unexpected about the text, so think beyond the obvious parallels and differences.

- **Trace**

  Choose an image—for example, birds, knives, or eyes—and trace that image throughout MACBETH.

  Sounds pretty easy, right? All you need to do is read the play, underline every appearance of a knife in *Macbeth,* and then list them in your essay in the order they appear, right? Well, not exactly. Your teacher doesn't want a simple catalog of examples. He or she wants to see you make *connections* between those examples—that's the difference between summarizing and analyzing. In the *Macbeth* example above, think about the different contexts in which knives appear in the play and to what effect. In *Macbeth,* there are real knives and imagined knives; knives that kill and knives that simply threaten. Categorize and classify your examples to give them some order. Finally, always keep the overall effect in mind. After you choose and analyze your examples, you should come to some greater understanding about the work, as well as your chosen image, symbol, or phrase's role in developing the major themes and stylistic strategies of that work.

- **Debate**

  Is the society depicted in 1984 *good for its citizens?*

  In this kind of essay, you're being asked to debate a moral, ethical, or aesthetic issue regarding the work. You might be asked to judge a character or group of characters (*Is Caesar responsible for his own demise?*) or the work itself (*Is* JANE EYRE *a feminist novel?*). For this kind of essay, there are two important points to keep in mind. First, don't simply base your arguments on your personal feelings and reactions. Every literary essay expects you to read and analyze the work, so search for evidence in the text. What do characters in *1984* have to say about the government of Oceania? What images does Orwell use that might give you a hint about his attitude toward the government? As in any debate, you also need to make sure that you define all the necessary terms before you begin to argue your case. What does it mean to be a "good" society? What makes a novel "feminist"? You should define your terms right up front, in the first paragraph after your introduction.

  Second, remember that strong literary essays make contrary and surprising arguments. Try to think outside the box. In the *1984* example above, it seems like the obvious answer would be no, the totalitarian society depicted in Orwell's novel is *not* good for its citizens. But can you think of any arguments for the opposite side? Even if your final assertion is that the novel depicts a cruel, repressive, and therefore harmful society, acknowledging and responding to the counterargument will strengthen your overall case.

5. WRITE THE INTRODUCTION

Your introduction sets up the entire essay. It's where you present your topic and articulate the particular issues and questions you'll be addressing. It's also where you, as the writer, introduce yourself to your readers. A persuasive literary essay immediately establishes its writer as a knowledgeable, authoritative figure.

An introduction can vary in length depending on the overall length of the essay, but in a traditional five-paragraph essay it should be no longer than one paragraph. However long it is, your introduction needs to:

- **Provide any necessary context.** Your introduction should situate the reader and let him or her know what to expect. What book are you discussing? Which characters? What topic will you be addressing?

- **Answer the "So what?" question.** Why is this topic important, and why is your particular position on the topic noteworthy? Ideally, your introduction should pique the reader's interest by suggesting how your argument is surprising or otherwise counterintuitive. Literary essays make unexpected connections and reveal less-than-obvious truths.

- **Present your thesis.** This usually happens at or very near the end of your introduction.

- **Indicate the shape of the essay to come.** Your reader should finish reading your introduction with a good sense of the scope of your essay as well as the path you'll take toward proving your thesis. You don't need to spell out every step, but you do need to suggest the organizational pattern you'll be using.

Your introduction should not:

- **Be vague.** Beware of the two killer words in literary analysis: *interesting* and *important*. Of course the work, question, or example is interesting and important—that's why you're writing about it!

- **Open with any grandiose assertions.** Many student readers think that beginning their essays with a flamboyant statement such as, "Since the dawn of time, writers have been fascinated with the topic of free will," makes them sound important and commanding. You know what? It actually sounds pretty amateurish.

- **Wildly praise the work.** Another typical mistake student writers make is extolling the work or author. Your teacher doesn't need to be told that "Shakespeare is perhaps the greatest writer in the English language." You can mention a work's reputation in passing—by referring to *The Adventures of Huckleberry Finn* as "Mark Twain's enduring classic," for example—but don't make a point of bringing it up unless that reputation is key to your argument.

- **Go off-topic.** Keep your introduction streamlined and to the point. Don't feel the need to throw in all kinds of bells and whistles in order to impress your reader—just get to the point as quickly as you can, without skimping on any of the required steps.

---

6. WRITE THE BODY PARAGRAPHS

Once you've written your introduction, you'll take the arguments you developed in step 4 and turn them into your body paragraphs. The organization of this middle section of your essay will largely be determined by the argumentative strategy you use, but no matter how you arrange your thoughts, your body paragraphs need to do the following:

- **Begin with a strong topic sentence.** Topic sentences are like signs on a highway: they tell the reader where they are and where they're going. A good topic sentence not only alerts readers to what issue will be discussed in the following paragraph but also gives them a sense of what argument will be made *about* that issue. "Rumor and gossip play an important role in *The Crucible*" isn't a strong topic sentence because it doesn't tell us very much. "The community's constant gossiping creates an environment that allows false accusations to flourish" is a much stronger topic sentence— it not only tells us *what* the paragraph will discuss (gossip) but *how* the paragraph will discuss the topic (by showing how gossip creates a set of conditions that leads to the play's climactic action).

- **Fully and completely develop a single thought.** Don't skip around in your paragraph or try to stuff in too much material. Body paragraphs are like bricks: each individual one needs to be strong and sturdy or the entire structure will collapse. Make sure you have really proven your point before moving on to the next one.

- **Use transitions effectively.** Good literary essay writers know that each paragraph must be clearly and strongly linked to the material around it. Think of each paragraph as a response to the one that precedes it. Use transition words and phrases such as *however, similarly, on the contrary, therefore,* and *furthermore* to indicate what kind of response you're making.

---

7. WRITE THE CONCLUSION

Just as you used the introduction to ground your readers in the topic before providing your thesis, you'll use the conclusion to quickly summarize the specifics learned thus far and then hint at the broader implications of your topic. A good conclusion will:

- **Do more than simply restate the thesis.** If your thesis argued that *The Catcher in the Rye* can be read as a Christian allegory, don't simply end your essay by saying, "And that is why *The Catcher in the Rye* can be read as a Christian allegory." If you've constructed your arguments well, this kind of statement will just be redundant.

- **Synthesize the arguments, not summarize them.** Similarly, don't repeat the details of your body paragraphs in your conclusion. The reader has already read your essay, and chances are it's not so long that they've forgotten all your points by now.

- **Revisit the "So what?" question.** In your introduction, you made a case for why your topic and position are important. You should close your essay with the same sort of gesture. What do your readers know now that they didn't know before? How will that knowledge help them better appreciate or understand the work overall?

- **Move from the specific to the general.** Your essay has most likely treated a very specific element of the work—a single character, a small set of images, or a particular passage. In your conclusion, try to show how this narrow discussion has wider implications for the work overall. If your essay on *To Kill a Mockingbird* focused on the character of Boo Radley, for example, you might want to include a bit in your conclusion about how he fits into the novel's larger message about childhood, innocence, or family life.

- **Stay relevant.** Your conclusion should suggest new directions of thought, but it shouldn't be treated as an opportunity to pad your essay with all the extra, interesting ideas you came up with during your brainstorming sessions but couldn't fit into the essay proper. Don't attempt to stuff in unrelated queries or too many abstract thoughts.

- **Avoid making overblown closing statements.** A conclusion should open up your highly specific, focused discussion, but it should do so without drawing a sweeping lesson about life or human nature. Making such observations may be part of the point of reading, but it's almost always a mistake in essays, where these observations tend to sound overly dramatic or simply silly.

A+ Essay Checklist

Congratulations! If you've followed all the steps we've outlined above, you should have a solid literary essay to show for all your efforts. What if you've got your sights set on an A+? To write the kind of superlative essay that will be rewarded with a perfect grade, keep the following rubric in mind. These are the qualities that teachers expect to see in a truly A+ essay. How does yours stack up?

- ✓ Demonstrates a thorough understanding of the book
- ✓ Presents an original, compelling argument
- ✓ Thoughtfully analyzes the text's formal elements
- ✓ Uses appropriate and insightful examples
- ✓ Structures ideas in a logical and progressive order
- ✓ Demonstrates a mastery of sentence construction, transitions, grammar, spelling, and word choice

Suggested Essay Topics

1. *Discuss the function of physical setting in* The Scarlet Letter. *What is the relationship between the book's events and the locations in which these events take place? Do things happen in the forest that could not happen in the town? What about time of day? Does night bring with it a set of rules that differs from those of the daytime?*

2. *Describe Chillingworth's "revenge." Why does he choose to torture Dimmesdale and Hester when he could simply reveal that he is Hester's husband? What does this imply about justice? About evil?*

3. *Discuss the function of the past in this novel. The narrator tells a two-hundred-year-old story that is taken from a hundred-year-old manuscript. Why does Hawthorne use a framing story for this novel rather than simply telling the story? Why are the events set in such distant history?*

4. *Children play a variety of roles in this novel. Pearl is both a blessing and a curse to Hester, and she seems at times to serve as Hester's conscience. The town children, on the other hand, are cruel and brutally honest about their opinion of Hester and Pearl. Why are children presented as more perceptive and more honest than adults? How do children differ from adults in their potential for expressing these perceptions?*

5. *Native Americans make a few brief and mysterious appearances in this novel. What role do they play? In what ways might their presence contribute to the furthering of the book's central themes?*

LITERARY ANALYSIS

A+ Student Essay

Is *The Scarlet Letter* a feminist novel?

Although *The Scarlet Letter* was written in 1850, long before the emergence of what we now refer to as feminism, the novel amounts to a spirited, pre-feminist defense of women and women's rights. Although modern readers might not immediately identify the tormented, cringing, sometimes self-loathing Hester Prynne as a feminist icon, that is exactly how Hawthorne portrays her. Whether directly or indirectly praising her behavior, Hawthorne holds her up as a model individual from whom both men and women should draw inspiration.

Hawthorne is not always straightforward in his depiction of Hester as a strong woman worthy of admiration. His tendency toward obfuscation, in combination with the now-archaic gender roles portrayed in *The Scarlet Letter,* misleads some readers into deciding that Hester is weak and her behavior inexplicable. But in fact, even those actions that might strike us as puzzlingly self-defeating become, upon closer reading, evidence of Hester's strength. We may wonder why Hester stoically wears the symbol of her adultery on her chest instead of ripping it off, but Hawthorne suggests that she appropriates the letter A, making it her own and turning it into a symbol not of her adultery, but of her many abilities. We may wonder why Hester remains in the midst of the people who have treated her so badly, but Hawthorne argues that by staying in town, she shows that she does not have to run away from her past in order to transcend it. Even when the narrator expresses disapproval of Hester's actions, an undercurrent of approval runs beneath it. For example, the narrator's purported condemnation of Hester's increasing coldness and self-reliance is mitigated by a strong sense that he understands and appreciates the reasons she has changed.

If Hawthorne is often reserved in his praise of Hester, however, he is just as often lavish with it. He portrays those who judge her, male and female alike, as coarse hypocrites. He turns our attention to Mistress Hibbins, forcing us to recognize the insanity of a society that tolerates an unrepentant, devil-worshipping witch on the one hand, yet banishes an adulterous woman on the other hand. He asks us to compare Hester's strength, openness, and loyalty with Dimmesdale's cowardly silence and Chillingworth's nearly psychotic quest for revenge. He has Dimmesdale state explicitly that adultery is practically meaningless compared to the evil of vengefulness, a statement that casts Hester as a martyr at the hands of society in general and Chillingworth in particular. Hawthorne stresses that in the face of unbearably cruel treatment, Hester responds with laudable strength and humility.

Of course, Hawthorne never would have used the word *feminist* to describe Hester Prynne. Yet if a modern reader described a feminist as someone who believes that women have rights, Hawthorne would likely agree that Hester fits the description. His tapestry of approval for Hester's actions, which he weaves from both quiet and bold colors, provides a picture of what strong pro-woman sentiment looked like in the days before feminism existed.

LITERARY ANALYSIS

GLOSSARY OF LITERARY TERMS

ANTAGONIST

The entity that acts to frustrate the goals of the *protagonist*. The antagonist is usually another *character* but may also be a non-human force.

ANTIHERO / ANTIHEROINE

A *protagonist* who is not admirable or who challenges notions of what should be considered admirable.

CHARACTER

A person, animal, or any other thing with a personality that appears in a *narrative*.

CLIMAX

The moment of greatest intensity in a text or the major turning point in the *plot*.

CONFLICT

The central struggle that moves the *plot* forward. The conflict can be the *protagonist*'s struggle against fate, nature, society, or another person.

FIRST-PERSON POINT OF VIEW

A literary style in which the *narrator* tells the story from his or her own *point of view* and refers to himself or herself as "I." The narrator may be an active participant in the story or just an observer.

HERO / HEROINE

The principal *character* in a literary work or *narrative*.

IMAGERY

Language that brings to mind sense-impressions, representing things that can be seen, smelled, heard, tasted, or touched.

MOTIF

A recurring idea, structure, contrast, or device that develops or informs the major *themes* of a work of literature.

NARRATIVE

A story.

NARRATOR

The person (sometimes a *character*) who tells a story; the *voice* assumed by the writer. The narrator and the author of the work of literature are not the same person.

PLOT

The arrangement of the events in a story, including the sequence in which they are told, the relative emphasis they are given, and the causal connections between events.

POINT OF VIEW

The *perspective* that a *narrative* takes toward the events it describes.

PROTAGONIST

The main *character* around whom the story revolves.

SETTING

The location of a *narrative* in time and space. Setting creates mood or atmosphere.

SUBPLOT

A secondary *plot* that is of less importance to the overall story but may serve as a point of contrast or comparison to the main plot.

SYMBOL

An object, *character,* figure, or color that is used to represent an abstract idea or concept. Unlike an *emblem,* a symbol may have different meanings in different contexts.

SYNTAX

The way the words in a piece of writing are put together to form lines, phrases, or clauses; the basic structure of a piece of writing.

THEME

A fundamental and universal idea explored in a literary work.

TONE

The author's attitude toward the subject or *characters* of a story or poem or toward the reader.

VOICE

An author's individual way of using language to reflect his or her own personality and attitudes. An author communicates voice through *tone, diction,* and *syntax.*

LITERARY ANALYSIS

A NOTE ON PLAGIARISM

Plagiarism—presenting someone else's work as your own—rears its ugly head in many forms. Many students know that copying text without citing it is unacceptable. But some don't realize that even if you're not quoting directly, but instead are paraphrasing or summarizing, *it is plagiarism* unless you cite the source.

Here are the most common forms of plagiarism:

- Using an author's phrases, sentences, or paragraphs without citing the source
- Paraphrasing an author's ideas without citing the source
- Passing off another student's work as your own

How do you steer clear of plagiarism? You should *always* acknowledge all words and ideas that aren't your own by using quotation marks around verbatim text or citations like footnotes and endnotes to note another writer's ideas. For more information on how to give credit when credit is due, ask your teacher for guidance or visit www.sparknotes.com.

Review & Resources

Quiz

1. In what century is the story of Hester Prynne set?

    A. The sixteenth century
    B. The seventeenth century
    C. The eighteenth century
    D. The nineteenth century

2. What is the occupation of the narrator of this story?

    A. Attorney
    B. Minister
    C. Land surveyor
    D. Customs officer

3. Where do Hester and Chillingworth live before coming to America?

    A. Amsterdam
    B. Paris
    C. Edinburgh
    D. Jamaica

4. With whom has Chillingworth been living before he appears in Boston?

    A. Another band of Puritans
    B. Native Americans
    C. Spanish settlers in Florida
    D. Canadian fur trappers

5. What is situated immediately outside the door of the prison in which Hester is kept?

    A. A rosebush
    B. A pine tree
    C. A gallows
    D. A graveyard

6. What item in the governor's mansion shows Hester a distorted reflection of herself?

   A. An antique mirror
   B. A suit of armor
   C. A stained-glass window
   D. The governor's eyeglasses

7. Which of the following is a method Dimmesdale uses to punish himself for his sins?

   A. Scourging or whipping
   B. Fasting
   C. Vigils (extended periods of wakefulness and/or prayer)
   D. All of the above

8. In what city do Hester and Pearl live?

   A. Salem
   B. Providence
   C. Boston
   D. Hartford

9. Who is Mistress Hibbins?

   A. The governor's sister
   B. Hester's mother
   C. Dimmesdale's aunt
   D. Chillingworth's second wife

10. How does Mistress Hibbins eventually die?

    A. She is strangled by Chillingworth.
    B. She wastes away in a diphtheria epidemic.
    C. She is executed publicly as a witch.
    D. Pearl puts a hex on her.

11. How does Hester support herself financially?

    A. As a prostitute
    B. As a seamstress
    C. As a nurse
    D. As a farmhand

12. Next to whom is Hester buried?

    A. Dimmesdale
    B. Chillingworth
    C. Pearl
    D. No one; her body is burned.

13. What natural phenomenon comes to symbolize both Dimmesdale's "sin" and Governor Winthrop's "virtue"?

    A. A lightning bolt
    B. A meteor
    C. A forest fire
    D. A flood

14. Why does Pearl not recognize her mother when she sees her with Dimmesdale in the forest?

    A. Hester has removed the scarlet letter.
    B. Hester has removed her cap to expose her long hair.
    C. Hester is not wearing her usual plain gray dress.
    D. Mistress Hibbins has cast a spell on Hester, changing her appearance.

15. How does Pearl acknowledge Dimmesdale as her father at his death?

    A. By calling him "father"
    B. By interrupting his sermon
    C. By kissing him
    D. By announcing that she has seen him with her mother

16. What mark can supposedly be seen on Dimmesdale's chest?

    A. A scarlet letter "A"
    B. A tattoo
    C. The mark of the devil
    D. A red rose

REVIEW & RESOURCES

17. How do Hester and Dimmesdale plan to escape their suffering?

    A.   By going to live with the Native Americans
    B.   By boarding a ship bound for Europe
    C.   By killing Chillingworth
    D.   By committing suicide

18. How does Pearl become wealthy?

    A.   She discovers pirates' treasure.
    B.   She marries the governor's son.
    C.   She inherits Chillingworth's estate and marries a nobleman.
    D.   She becomes a famous actress and dancer.

19. Where does the narrator first encounter Hester Prynne's story?

    A.   He finds a manuscript in the attic of the Salem Custom-House.
    B.   He hears it from an elderly aunt.
    C.   He hears it from one of the old men who work at the Salem Custom-House.
    D.   It comes to him in a dream.

20. What item of clothing does Hester make for Governor Winthrop?

    A.   A cloak for his swearing-in
    B.   A nightcap
    C.   A pair of gloves
    D.   A winter hat

21. What color of clothing does Hester always wear?

    A.   Scarlet
    B.   White
    C.   Black
    D.   Gray

22. Where do Hester and Pearl live?

    A. In the poorhouse
    B. In an abandoned cottage on the outskirts of Boston
    C. In the forest
    D. In the house of Roger Chillingworth

23. What does Chillingworth pretend to be?

    A. A minister
    B. A doctor
    C. A madman
    D. A scholar

24. What does Hester's letter "A" eventually come to represent to the townspeople?

    A. "Able"
    B. "Alone"
    C. "Avaricious"
    D. "Absolutely Admirable"

25. Why does the narrator lose his job in the customhouse?

    A. He is incompetent.
    B. He spends too much time writing when he should be working.
    C. The other inspectors dislike him personally.
    D. A new president is elected, and a new chief customs officer is appointed.

Suggestions for Further Reading

BARLOWE, JAMIE. *The Scarlet Mob of Scribblers: Rereading Hester Prynne*. Carbondale: Southern Illinois University Press, 2000.

BAYM, NINA. THE SCARLET LETTER: *A Reading*. Boston: Twayne Publishers, 1986.

BELL, MILLICENT, ed. *Hawthorne and the Real: Bicentennial Essays*. Columbus, OH: Ohio State University Press, 2005.

BERCOVITCH, SACVAN. *The Office of the Scarlet Letter*. Baltimore: Johns Hopkins University Press, 1992.

BERLANT, LAUREN. *The Anatomy of National Fantasy: Hawthorne, Utopia, and Everyday Life*. Chicago: University of Chicago Press, 1991.

BLOOM, HAROLD, ed. *Nathaniel Hawthorne's* THE SCARLET LETTER. New York: Chelsea House Publishers, 2007.

JOHNSON, CLAUDIA D. *Understanding* THE SCARLET LETTER: *A Student Casebook to Issues, Sources, and Historical Documents*. Westport, CT: Greenwood Press, 1995.

KESTERSON, DAVID B., ed. *Critical Essays on Hawthorne's* THE SCARLET LETTER. Boston: G. K. Hall, 1988.

MATTHIESSEN, F. O. *American Renaissance: Art and Expression in the Age of Emerson and Whitman*. Oxford: Oxford University Press, 1941.

THICKSTUN, MARGARET. *Fictions of the Feminine: Puritan Doctrine and the Representation of Women*. Ithaca, NY: Cornell University Press, 1988.